1947 EUROPE FROM A DUFFEL BAG

1947 EUROPE FROM A DUFFEL BAG

Charles Cutting

To order additional copies of this book, contact:
Xlibris Corporation
1-888-795-4274
www.Xlibris.com
Orders@Xlibris.com
35219

CONTENTS

CHAPTER 1

Family background shapes one's future

This narrative was completed in the year 2005 as I passed seventy-five years of age. The contents were drawn from my memory—a log that I kept in 1947-48 and a collection of photographs and postcards collected on that long-ago adventure.

It is interesting to speculate on the various elements that propel a young man on such a trip away from the safe harbor of one's childhood. I grew up living with several California families that had common characteristics: they were all people of varied backgrounds of travel; they all spent substantial time reading and discussing world events of the day.

My paternal great-grandfather migrated from Haverhill, New Hampshire, to Riceville, Iowa, in the early 1800s. This man, Charles Douglass Cutting (1834-1926), became a successful farmer and state legislator. However, the long, frigid Iowa winters made his advancing years painful, from the effects of arthritis. Several relatives and neighbors had already migrated to California, and their descriptions of the beautiful Santa Clara County persuaded him to migrate further west.

In 1892, Great-grandfather Cutting bought a five-acre fruit orchard near the corner of Hamilton and Leigh Avenues in Campbell, California. In addition, he leased an apple orchard in Soquel.

My grandfather, Frank Harvey Cutting (1872-1964), was one of five sons born and raised on the family farm near Riceville, Iowa. At age twenty, he also left the farm in Iowa to join his family, who had gone ahead to California.

My grandmother, Clara Jane Snavely Cutting (1877-1962), was born in Indiana but moved to Iowa as a young girl to work on a newspaper and as a helper in the Cutting household. With the family's move to California, she also came west with her widowed sister, my great-aunt Cora, and they also settled in Campbell.

Once my grandfather Frank (Francis Cutting) moved west, he worked long hours on the home farm while completing a teaching degree at the San Jose State Normal School. He found he disliked teaching, so after working two years in this profession, he quit and returned to farming. His real love was oil painting, and at age forty-five, he sold his farm interests and became a landscape painter for the remainder of his ninety-one years.

As a child, I often traveled with my grandfather on camping trips to Yosemite and Pacific Grove-Big Sur areas. At an early age, I was able to roam the open country and became self-reliant while he worked for an hour or so at his easel, engrossed with his canvas. From age six onward, I spent more and more time exploring on my own. I think this was the inception of my interest in exploration and travel.

The early days

In the years 1937 and 1939, I lived with my aunt Belle and uncle Ralph Hain. They lived on a ranch twenty-five miles from the town of Hollister in the hardscrabble backcountry near the Pinnacles National Monument in Northern California.

My aunt Belle graduated from Stanford University with a master's degree in German. (This was a feat almost unthinkable for a young woman in the early 1900s.) Her husband, my Uncle Ralph, had grown up on a ranch, and his school had ended with the sixth grade. With this great disparity in education, they lived for over fifty years in harmonious union.

He was a soldier in World War I and went to France as a teamster, hauling supplies and ammunition to the front in the Battle of Belleau Wood. On his return to California, he tended cattle on ranches. Later during the Depression, he worked as a gold dredge mechanic in Sonora and alternately as a park ranger in the Pinnacles National Monument.

My aunt Belle was the only teacher in the Jefferson one-room school of eight students. She had a system of teaching that allowed a student who completed his or her assignments to sit in on a class of an upper grade. I was very interested in geography and history and was able to work far ahead in these subjects. In our old ranch house, we had a radio that operated off a car battery, and each evening we listened to fifteen minutes of the nine o'clock news as the war clouds of World War II developed. My uncle told me stories of his army days in Europe in 1918 while my aunt, with her knowledge of German, translated Hitler's speeches of the day.

Genealogy

On my mother's side of the family, there were several generations of sea captains, who sailed out of Yarmouth, Nova Scotia, and Eastport, Maine. My maternal grandfather's grandfather sailed the *Eagle*—his own forty two foot vessel—from Yarmouth, Nova Scotia, to San Francisco in 1852. Once settled in California, he traded his boat for a track of land that ran from the East Bay waterfront back in to the hills behind Milpitas. He built his own boat landing near Warm Springs on the east shore of San Francisco Bay. Warm Springs Landing was destroyed in an 1864 earthquake, and he then bought the present-day Dixon Landing site. From these locations, he sailed farm produce to the gold miners in Sacramento and across the bay to San Francisco.

His son was the captain of a ship that was lost off Cape Horn. The son of this lost sailor was my grandfather. He did not follow the sea but worked in the gold mines of the mother lode and later became a builder in Madera, California. Still later, he moved to San Francisco to help rebuild the city after the 1906 earthquake.

In 1920, he bought a sheep ranch at Spy Rock, north of Laytonville in Northern California. His end came when he hired a young man who needed work. A short time after this youth came to work for my grandfather, they went to clean out a mountain spring on the property. The young man picked up my grandfather's rifle and shot him in the back, killing him. Later when the posse rode this man down, he said, "God made me do it." He was a deserter from the U.S. Navy and was sent to San Quentin Prison for life.

These events all occurred before I was born, so I never had an opportunity to know my maternal grandfather. One item that connected me to this event happened in 1940. My mother was a schoolteacher in Sunnyvale, California, and one day on my return from a friend's house, I heard my mother loudly swearing at a man who had come to our home. This was very unusual as it was the only time in my life that I ever heard my mother swear, much less yell.

Years later, I learned what had occurred. The man represented a group of "do-gooders" that were trying to get my grandfather's murderer released from San Quentin. In those days, it was necessary to get the murdered man's next of kin to okay this. My mother was having none of it.

In 1995, I went to San Quentin to inquire as to the end of this man but was told that no records remain before about 1940 due to a fire that burned the records building. So his final fate is a mystery.

CHAPTER 2

Building a nest egg for travel

The last three and one-half years of high school, I lived with my grandparents while completing my education. I had just turned seventeen when I graduated from high school in June of 1947 and decided that I was not ready for college.

I wanted to see the world before settling down to the academic regime. I had spent my summers working for a trucking company since I was thirteen. This was a time before forklifts were in use, so all the work of loading trucks was done by hand. Trucking companies would hire high school boys as swampers to work out in the fields, loading boxes of produce.

We would ride out with a driver into a pear, peach, or apricot orchard, and the driver would unhook his trailer and drop two of us off and drive his truck cab away. The pair of us would load seventeen tons of forty-pound fruit boxes off the ground and stack them five high on the bed of the trailer. It was hard, grueling work, but the pay was high for a teenager. At the end of the summer's work, I would be in prime physical condition. It was a fascinating world of men that was far removed from my God-fearing grandparents' lifestyle.

These swearing, hard-drinking truck drivers were honorable, hardworking gentlemen, earning their livelihood at hard labor. When I was sixteen, I could crank up, double-clutch, and drive a diesel semitruck with the education gleaned from these good old kings of the road.

With the money earned, I paid much of my room, clothing, and board in all the years that I lived with my grandparents. My father had been killed in a bus accident when I was twelve, and the insurance money came to five thousand dollars. This sum lasted from age twelve to twenty-one and covered my room, board, medical needs, and schooling through the years.

My grandparents were not wealthy, so they said if I could pay part of my expenses, I would have some left when I reached the age of twenty-one.

Now, as a parent, I know that they must have paid most of my requirements and did not charge me nearly enough. (I had two thousand dollars left when I reached my majority. I now live on the property that I bought with this money when I was twenty-one.)

These early days of hard work taught me to be frugal and to meet my obligations in life. Today, in this time of plenty, my children still do not fully understand the events that shaped my life, forged in the Great Depression. All these events helped prepare me for the adventures that lay ahead.

In 1947, with my high school graduation behind me, I was ready to move out onto the open road. During the last two years of high school, I had been dreaming and scheming of somehow making my way around the world. I spent the summer of 1947 working once again for Nelson Brothers Trucking Company. In my box of mementoes, I have a pay stub for eighty-two hours for one week of heavy work in that long-ago summer.

By mid-August of that year, I had saved a total of four hundred dollars above my board and room requirements. These funds I put into the safety of a local bank. With this money as a backup, I was ready to make my way east on my travel adventure. In addition to the bank account, my possessions included two new pairs of Levi's, stout hiking boots, three pairs of underwear, one pair of slacks and shirt to match, a jackknife, small personal odds and ends, sweater, a waterproof jacket, three shirts, several road maps, plus an army surplus barracks/duffel bag. I purchased the bag for fifty cents from a San Jose Army-Navy surplus store.

In addition, my aunt Leona lent me a small camera that completed my equipment for the trip east. How far east I would get was a big question!

CHAPTER 3

October 2, 1947, On the road

October 2, 1947, I arose in the dark at 2:30 a.m., said good-by to my worried grandparents, put half of fifty dollars in my duffel bag, the remainder into my wallet; and I was off on my adventure.

I hoisted my bag onto my shoulder, walked down a dark alley, cut across the railroad tracks, and arrived in the Nelson Brothers truck yard. In the darkness, the low rumble of a semitruck warming up gave the assurance that I had arrived on time. Truck driver Carl Myers threw my bag up into the cab and then walked back to sign out of the dispatch office. On his return, he said, "Why don't you take her out?"

I slid behind the wheel and eased the truck, loaded with sacked cement, out onto the highway headed for Sacramento. In the darkness, we drove north through Oakland; and as we approached Crockett Bridge, daylight began to break in the eastern sky. Moments later, we dropped downhill to cross the Carquinez Strait and drove into a pea-soup fog out of San Pablo Bay. The traffic slowed, and I downshifted to a crawl seeing only the taillights of the car in front. A few minutes passed, and we began our climb up the ridge of hills that divides the Bay Area from the Sacramento Valley. The fog soon dissipated with altitude, and the rising sun blinded us with its radiance. Reaching the far side of the ridge, we wound down into the clear, cold valley below.

Another half hour and we stopped in Fairfield for hot coffee and breakfast. Carl insisted on paying the bill as he joked and said, "I would never make it to Europe." He then took over the wheel and drove on to his dumpsite on the west side of Sacramento. We shook hands, and he wished me the best of luck.

I scrambled down out of the cab with my duffel bag on my shoulder. Now I began to feel the impact of being at once alone and on the move into the total unknown. It was both frightening and, in the same moment, exhilarating.

I rode east on a city bus for a dime and caught a glimpse of the California State Capitol as we rolled past. On the east side of Sacramento, I arrived at Highway 50. I had hitchhiked enough in the last few years to realize bumming in a city is not productive. There is also the added peril of a cop who will hassle any teenager who is obviously not on his way to a local school.

On the east side of town, I hitched a ride toward the Sierra Nevada Mountains. The drive took us on a gradual rise toward the mountains. On either side of the roadway were miles of rock slag created by the gold-mining dredges that laid waste to the foothills. The dredges closed down with the start of World War II, but their devastation will last for centuries. In little time, we arrived in Placerville where my first car ride ended.

This town, also called Hangtown, was a rip-roaring mining town in the early days of the California gold rush. Lots of plaques and relics of the past were posted throughout town. There was time for lunch and a short stroll through the old town to read inscriptions of gold-rush days.

Once again out on the road, I soon caught a ride going to South Lake Tahoe. En route we passed over the 7,392-foot Echo Summit before sighting the cerulean blue of the mountain lake in the afternoon sun. It was now 4:00 p.m., and I had reached my first goal of the trip.

Pinewoods reach all the way down to the water here in Bijou Park. I surveyed several places to stay and settled on a room at Earhart's Lake View Cottages in the village. The room was rustic but had a single bed, a double bed, shower with both hot and cold water, plus an indoor toilet. The cost was two dollars for a night. I unloaded my barracks bag on the double bed to survey my possessions and then repack it for the next day's journey. I began to feel the effects of a long day and decided to lie down and take a nap until time for supper. I crashed and did not wake up until seven the next morning. I was completely refreshed and had saved the price of an evening meal. Thus ended my first twenty-four hours on the road to Europe at a total cost of two dollars and sixty cents.

I arose and took a hot shower, shaved, dressed, and walked down the highway and located an all-night diner. A hot breakfast of bacon, eggs, and hash browns put my spirits on high. With my camera in hand, I walked down to the water's edge to take some photos. Here I discovered an older man already engaged in photography. In a few minutes, I discovered that he was a fellow doctor of my great-uncle Jimmy. He gave me some pointers on the use of my camera that, unfortunately, I did not retain.

When he discovered that I was off for Europe at seventeen, he made me an offer: If I would drop the trip, he would sell me his small lakeside cabin for my four hundred dollars. He was the first of many well-intentioned people who would try to talk me out of my trip into the unknown. We talked for a few more minutes and after saying "no thanks," I was on my way back to pick up my bag and continue my journey.

At ten a.m., I was picked up by two young men driving a small pickup truck. I rode in the open truck bed, and it was a harrowing ride over the mountains that ended with a steep drop down into the state of Nevada. The road was called the Kings Canyon Road, and it started at Spooner Summit and ended in the outskirts of Carson City. In the days of the silver strike in Virginia City, all the machinery for the mines came from San Francisco by freight wagons. The road we passed over was a dirt trail left from those early-wagon days. The view was spectacular; the vista spread one hundred miles and more out across Eagle Valley and the Nevada desert beyond. The driver was in a great hurry, and we threw clouds of dirt and gravel over the steep embankments as we swept down the hairpin road. I had to hang on with all my strength as we bucked and skidded from side to side down the steep east escarpment of the Sierra Nevadas.

On arrival in Carson City, the driver was proud of his wheelwork and let me know that we had cut off thirty to forty miles from the regular-paved Highway 50.

I thanked the driver for the lift but was happy to be safe and out of his vehicle on solid ground once again. When hitchhiking, the type and ability of the driver is always a grab bag of fate. I located a gas station and went into the restroom to wash the mixture of dirt and sweat from my face.

Out on the street again, I located the Nevada State Museum. This building had been built in the 1800s as the U.S. Mint of Nevada. They had an excellent collection of gold coins, the first old airplane to land in Carson City, a replica of a silver mine, and lots of memorabilia of bygone days.

I ate a light lunch and was back on the edge of Highway 50 by one thirty. My luck was poor, and I didn't catch a ride until four in the afternoon. I had developed a method to make the wait at roadside a little less fatiguing. Standing in the hot sun for long periods of time takes infinite patience. On the roadside there is always a lot of debris and with a little search, one can find the necessary material for a seat. Two broken bits of board do the trick nicely. You hold one short board vertical while forming a tee with the other piece. Now sit down gingerly with the feet wide apart, and the semblance of a three-legged stool is the net result. When a car appears on the horizon, you stand up and the bits of wood fall to the ground, out of sight. This works well as the psychology of the road dictates that the hitchhiker should stand, appear presentable, and eager for a ride.

Four p.m. and a car with New York plates pulled to a stop alongside my location. Another edict of the road is that the driver who picks you up is almost always bored and wants someone to talk to. If you step in out of the hot sun and promptly go to sleep, you are apt to be discharged at the next stop sign. So intelligent conversation is a must; and though heavy with fatigue, one must appear alert.

The New York driver and I were soon in conversation. The road trailed eastward over mile upon mile of flat high desert. Now and again, low rocky ridges bisected the moonscape scenery. Often, when passing through these mountainous outcroppings of rock, the entrance to a mine could be seen with its signature of weathered mine tailings. The road, through these passes, has been straightened over the years for high-speed driving.

On occasion, signs of the old path of wagon tracks that marked the trails of yesteryear could be seen. Another interesting sight was that of farms way out in middesert. They were fed water by narrow concrete canals. Where this water originated in this desolate land was hard to fathom. These farms seemed to be operating on an experimental basis.

Sunset swept upon us with a beautiful display of red, gold, and green hues in the evening sky. In a short time, we arrived in Austin, Nevada. This ended my trip for the day, as it was the driver's destination. My benefactor found an expensive place to stay, and I walked through town until I located a rundown cabin for two dollars. After washing up I met my friend, and we located the only place in town open for dinner.

Completing a hearty meal, he went into the side room to play roulette. I talked to a shady young lady who told me her life story over several cups of coffee. Later she left to take care of a rough-looking character, who was in a great hurry to get her upstairs. I watched my driving partner lose a steady stream of money at the gaming table, and, not wishing to participate, I said good night. We agreed to meet the next morning at 5:45 a.m.

CHAPTER 4

October 3, 1947, Crossing the Nevada desert

I arose early to meet my driver, and we were on the road by 5:30 a.m. He nursed a hangover as he groused about his night of monetary losses. The highway was a repeat of yesterday's travel through mile after mile of sagebrush flats broken by an occasional barren ridge.

We passed through one more cleft in the rock that often appeared on rounding a bend in the road. In this pass, we came into the ancient silver-mining town of Eureka, Nevada. This ended our association as he had business in this town.

Hunger had set in, and so we stopped together for breakfast. There was only one place open at that early hour, so our choice was easy. It was filled with the type of characters one would have expected in the 1800s. The man that I sat down next to was a gambler. While I ate, he thumbed and rethumbed through his night's IOUs. His young face was drawn and highlighted with heavy circles under his dark eyes. He wore wrinkled black clothes and sported a well-trimmed blond mustache and goatee. A Western movie could not have provided the look of a more realistic card shark.

I ate my pancakes and watched him out of the corner of my eye. He drank several cups of hot black coffee; and all the while, his fingers were never still. My partner of yesterday was eating a huge breakfast as I departed. With my duffel bag hoisted on my shoulder, I strolled down the almost-deserted block that represented the entire town. I was ready for a fresh start down the highway.

On my walk toward the east end of town, I passed a man who matched the weathered gray bench he was sitting on. Thinking he might know something of history, I stopped to visit. He said that he had lived here and in the surrounding country for the past sevety-nine years.

Across the street from our location was a large brick building with a huge hole in the side. He explained that thieving miners had blown the breach into the building. This event occurred just as the mining boom failed, and the building was abandoned and was never repaired.

Another fascinating item he narrated was that the interior maple lumber for this old, decaying building had been brought from the East Coast around Cape Horn by sailing ship. Arriving in San Francisco, the cargo of boards was then freighted across the Nevada desert by mule wagons. He concluded with the statement that he had prospected all his life but always failed to find his El Dorado.

I felt my visiting time was up, and I moved on to the edge of town to continue my journey. I stood in the warmth of the rising sun on the edge of the interstate and waited. After a few minutes, a large four-door sedan drew to a stop alongside. In a moment, my bag and I were loaded in the rear seat, and we drove off. In the front seat, a middle-aged couple asked my destination, and I said New York City. The driver, who I took to be the husband, was interested and friendly but it soon became apparent that the wife was not happy.

It was obvious that she did not want me to join them. I tried to put her at ease with the story of my life and my plan for this trip, but she was obviously uncomfortable. We made a short lunch stop in the copper mining town of Ely, Nevada. While we ate, it developed that they were on their way to Ohio. The thought of completing such a long stretch on my journey east was very appealing.

On departure from Ely, the highway bent northward into Utah. Passing the Bonneville Salt Flats near Wendover, Utah, we could see a gathering of men and machines out on the flat desert. Later I discovered that John Cobb was in the process of trying for a world speed record with his race car, the Railton Mobil Special. Cobb hoped to reach 400 mph but so far, 394.2 was his top speed run.

We continued toward Salt Lake City, and as we talked, it developed that the lady up front was convinced that I was on the lam from some criminal offence. I tried to allay her fears but to no avail. Late in the afternoon, we passed along the south shore of the Great Salt Lake. After a short drive, we had arrived in the heart of the Mormon capitol.

The couple planned to lie over for the night, with an early departure the following morning. I left them so I could search for less-expensive lodging. The husband said they would pick me up at 5:00 a.m. the next morning at a certain intersection.

I found a place to stay the night in the Plandome Hotel. Cost was one dollar, without bath. A penciled note in my trip diary states "a real first-class hole in the wall." Not withstanding a note on their business card that stated, "Your Recommending Us is Doing Your Friend a Favor." Ha! Ha! It didn't take long to clean up using the small sink with a minuscule piece of cracked, used soap.

I walked to the Mormon Temple and was impressed by its beautiful architecture. The building was started in 1853 and was not completed until 1893. The high point is the 210-foot east center tower with a statue of the Angel Moroni gilded with pure gold leaf on the very top.

In a museum close at hand was located the first log cabin that was built in Salt Lake City.

Later I paid one dollar and twenty cents for a supper of breaded veal cutlets and a glass of milk. This cost was outrageous, but hunger had overcome my inner reticence, and I paid without complaint. In the evening, I walked through the business district and discovered a large crowd standing outside a department store. Thinking there might be a robbery in progress, I rushed to join the people peering through the display window.

To my surprise, there was a small flicker of greenish light illuminating the first television set that I have ever seen. (Today we take TV for granted as part of our daily lives, but it is hard to describe the incredulous look of the men and women viewing this phenomenon for the first time in their lives.) I then returned to my hotel room and was soon lost in the sleep of one who is completely exhausted.

CHAPTER 5

October 4, 1947, Left in the lurch

Up without breakfast, I was soon standing on the appointed street corner to pick up my ride with my benefactors of the previous day. It was not a great surprise that after an hour in the cold morning air, they did not appear. The lady had been very uncertain about my past, and I was sure she told her husband, "No way do we pick that punk kid up again."

It was 5:30 a.m. and I decided to return to my room. The key still lay on the bed waiting for the arrival of the maids. In moments, my shoes were off; and with a spread pulled over me, I was fast asleep once again. Nine a.m. was the official checkout time; and a minute or two early, I was out the door and soon located a breakfast café.

Completing my repast, I boarded a city bus, headed toward the east side of the city, to start my day's work on Highway 40. This turned out to be a bad day for hitchhiking. It was hot and dusty with little traffic. Lunchtime showed a net gain of twelve miles. I decided to skip lunch and to continue on.

Dust devils swirled around, and the heat made me drowsy as I stood hour after hour by the roadside. The arrival of a battered old pickup brought an end to hours of boredom, and I was pleased to be on my way once again. The grizzled old driver wanted to talk, but the hours of standing in the sun caused me to be so sleepy that I just could not carry on a conversation. As I had mentioned earlier, this is not acceptable manners for a hitchhiker. My head soon rested on my chest as I slept the miles away.

Once when we crossed over the 8,000-foot Daniels Pass, I awoke but soon, I was sleeping once again. The driver came to a place where a dirt road led off into the wilderness; and he woke me to announce, "I'm a sheep herder, and this is where I turn off the main road."

I scrambled down with my bag and looked around the surrounding country. There was already a chill in the high desert air as I took stock of my situation. I had skipped lunch and now dinner was a loss also. My location was near the summit of a long grade that wound up from a valley below. There didn't seem to be any traffic, and I began to realize that I would have a hard, hungry night ahead.

In the arid sagebrush country, the night came with a rush to be followed with intense cold. Just before darkness, there had been the passage of two separate cars. They did not slow in the least and even seemed to accelerate as they spied this lone figure far out in the wilderness. I needed to make arrangements for a long night.

Up ahead I discovered a small culvert that passed under the narrow two-lane road. Then came the idea. I climbed down off the roadway and started pulling grass and stuffing it into the culvert pipe. It did not take long to block the pipe to keep the wind from passing through. In the gathering darkness, I soon had a bed of grass to lie upon just inside the pipe entrance. Next, I unpacked the clothes from my bag and put on an extra pair of pants and sweater. The last of my gear I spread out on top of the dry grass to provide more insulation from the metal pipe. With nightfall, there wasn't a breath of air movement, and the temperature dropped rapidly. The stars appeared in the millions in the coal black night. The mournful howl of a coyote broke the stillness. I was not frightened but felt a strong surge of loneliness as I crawled into my burrow. Within minutes, the corrugated rings of the pipe began to bite onto my backside, and the chill began to seep into my bones. I considered crawling out to run in place to build up body heat.

Then, far to the west down the highway, I could hear the motor of a vehicle in slow ascent approaching. In a flash, I had scrambled out of my hole and was standing at the roadside. The headlight beams caught me in full glare as I stood with my thumb out for a ride. A snap-on tool truck pulled up alongside and stopped. When I opened the door, I made a quick explanation to the driver that all my gear was down in the pipe beneath the road where I had holed up for the night. Would he wait while I retrieved my clothes? What a relief when he said "no problem."

In the blessed warmth of his cab, we were soon in discussion of world events and life's problems and joys. The truck hummed along through the cold, starlit night, and we soon arrived in the small town of Duchesne. I located a hotel room for one dollar and later had my supper in the downstairs dining room for ninety cents.

Once back in my room, the fear of being robbed while I slept struck my mind with a vengeance. What triggered this intense unease, I had no idea. I divided my money and hid one-half in each shoe. Next, I hid the shoes under a dresser and then completed my preparations by propping a chair under the doorknob. The fire escape consisted of a knotted rope that was tied to the steam radiator that could be dropped out the window to the street, one story below. In a few minutes, my concerns of robbery and fire were lost as sleep overtook my weary body.

CHAPTER 6

October 5, 1947, The fight

Out on the road by 7:00 a.m., the truck driver and I were soon making good progress. In a few miles, we passed Fort Duchesne. The driver said that the first regiment of troops stationed here were the Negro or Buffalo Soldiers in the 1870s.

We were soon crossing the border of Colorado. We were now in high sagebrush country that had recently been the location of a Wild West oil strike. A gravel road cut diagonally across Highway 40. A small wooden sign pointed to the shantytown of Artesia. In the distance could be seen the derricks of a forest of oil wells. Located on this intersection was a small tar paper building with TAVERN written in big letters above a large plate glass window. My snap-on-tool-truck driver stopped long enough to let me out. He then turned down the gravel road headed in the direction of the oil derricks that could be seen far out across the flats. I hopped down with my duffel bag and called a good-bye to the driver as he sped away.

A building housing a bar was on the far side of the road. As I stood looking back down the road for a possible ride, I heard a great commotion. Turning toward the noise, I saw two men tumbling out the front door of the bar and raising a cloud of dust as they continued a vicious fistfight. Rolling around on the hard dirt didn't seem to satisfy them adequately, so they rose up and wrestled and pushed one another until they crashed into the plate glass window. The pane came out in a shower of shards, with a bang.

The barkeeper rushed out with a blackjack and began to beat on the two contestants. Within moments, other drunks from the bar entered the fray. An Indian driving by skidded his Model A to a halt and jumped into the fracas.

I stood spellbound across the street, watching as the barkeeper laid out someone with his blackjack. Several of the townspeople stood around the edges of the battle and laughed and called encouragement to the combatants.

I was caught completely by surprise when a Colorado state trooper rolled up alongside where I was standing. He climbed out of his vehicle and strutted over to my position with a stern expression and proceeded to give me a five-minute lecture informing me that hitchhiking was not allowed in the state of Colorado.

This task completed, he leisurely climbed back in his car and drove over to the fight across the street. By this time, the bartender and the Indian were the only two combatants still upright. Some discussion and note taking followed before the patrolman returned to his vehicle. He soon disappeared as he wheeled west, down the highway.

A few minutes passed while I continued to hitchhike—all the while keeping a wary eye on the possible return of the patrolman. In a short time, a fellow picked me up; and we were soon speeding east. We discussed the similarity of the gold-rush days and this wild time of an oil-rush boom.

This man had a great laugh when I told him of my lecture from the patrolman. He was an interesting fellow and regaled me with stories of shooting grizzly bears and a torrid love affair with the niece of Henry Ford.

On this ride in his pickup truck, an event occurred that renewed my view of the goodness of mankind. We were traveling fast although the road was quite rough in spots. Transiting one of these spots of broken pavement, unknown to us, my barracks/duffel bag and a spare tire from the rear bed of the truck flew out onto the road. A driver headed in the opposite direction saw our gear hit the highway. He not only stopped and retrieved our articles but also turned around and raced after us.

Our first indication that anything was amiss was when he tailgated us blowing his horn and motioning us to pull over. Our first reaction was one of alarm. We are far out on a desolate section of highway where holdups might easily occur. My driver pulled a pistol from his glove compartment and laid it on the seat between us. My anxiety was evidenced by the feel of a pounding heart. His preparations completed, we pulled to the side of the road.

Our relief and reward was the recovery of our missing articles. Oh, what a happy ending! If it had not been for this good benefactor, I wonder if I would have continued on my journey. Not only would I have lost my extra clothes and operating cash but, most important, I would have lost my passport!

After this event, there was little realization of the passage of time. We drove on in silence. We continued to ascend the western slope of the Rocky

Mountains toward the Continental Divide. We arrived in Steamboat Springs in semidarkness at 7:00 p.m.

There was a lighted plaque in the city square that proclaimed the city name was derived from its springs that bubble and whistle in the early morning. The city fathers claimed the sound was reminiscent of the steamboats of the old Mississippi River trade.

I started looking for lodging and discovered the only single room left in town was located in Hotel Harbor. This place was touted to be the town's best and was indeed fancy. My room had a private bath, a telephone, and a writing desk; it certainly represented the lap of luxury for a cost of two dollars and fifty cents.

I had hitchhiked 234 miles since leaving Duchesne, Utah, in the morning. I was ready for bed. To make up for the high cost of the room, I decided to skip supper and, instead, ate an apple from the front desk for my repast. A long soak in the hot bath soon had me ready for the sleep of the exhausted traveler.

CHAPTER 7

October 6, 1947,

Across the Continental Divide

Six a.m. and I was up and had completed a big breakfast. A few minutes later, I was on the edge of Steamboat Springs looking for a ride. Luck was on my side as the first car to arrive stopped and picked me up.

We soon crossed the Continental Divide and wound our way down the eastern side of the Rocky Mountains. The view from Rabbit Ears Pass (9,425 feet) was truly spectacular. Fall had turned the mantle of quaking aspens gold.

We soon crossed the Colorado River and then paralleled the Blue River all the while surrounded by high craggy mountains.

My driver turned out to be most interesting. He had been an operative in counterintelligence in Germany during World War II, and I found his stories fascinating.

The past seven years he had been constantly on the move throughout the world. Now at age thirty-one, he was returning to marry and settle down in his hometown of Denver. The miles flew past as he discussed his philosophy of life in its many aspects.

Noontime arrived and we were in Denver. I thanked my driver and off-loaded my duffel bag and set out in search of the local YMCA. After a short streetcar ride I found myself in front of a six-story brick Y in the heart of Denver.

I rented a room with two single beds and another resident already in place. This fellow seemed a strange grouch, so I took my valuables down to the office safe and left for the afternoon.

For the price of one nickel, I was able to ride a streetcar out to old Denver and return. On the outbound trip, I sat next to a postal employee. One never thinks of all the ins and outs of a job until the opportunity to talk at length with an employee is available. His stories of misdirected mail were hilarious.

I spent the afternoon puttering around, buying two rolls of film and an exposure chart for my camera. (I did not realize that all the film that I had sent home to my grandparents was of no use because of my lack of understanding of f-stops and shutter speeds. Fortunately, after this day, my relatives began to receive a few usable exposed rolls of film.) In the evening, I returned for dinner at the YMCA.

One disturbing reoccurrence began to become a real nuisance. For some reason, I was having an average of six nosebleeds each day. Not only is this trait inconvenient but it also puts people off in a most decided way. Other than having several handkerchiefs on hand, there was not much I could do but hope it would soon end. (After two weeks, this malady ended and never returned.)

CHAPTER 8

October 7, 1947, On to Pike's Peak

I decided on an early start, so I was up and eating a light breakfast by 6:00 a.m. A fifteen-minute streetcar ride ended on the outskirts of town. I stood on the side of the highway that turned due south. I was in luck as the third car that came along stopped and picked me up. This man was on the road to Pueblo and was very fatigued. He wanted to know if I could drive while he took a nap. More good luck; what a pleasure it was to drive a brand new 1947 Ford Deluxe automobile. The owner spent his time snoring while I enjoyed the sights along the highway. Arriving at my destination, Colorado Springs, I returned the car to the rested owner.

I had always wanted to take a trip up Pike's Peak, and now was my opportunity. Once again, I located the YMCA for a room. I found a tourist agency and bought a ticket that would take me up the Peak by cog train and return by auto. The trip left at two in the afternoon. Having time to spare, I struck up a conversation with a gentleman in the lobby of the Y. He had been stationed in Adak, Alaska, during the war and had some interesting photographs of his military days on the island. Since it was lunchtime, we discussed army life while looking for a restaurant.

Before leaving California, my family doctor had given me prescriptions for a series of shots necessary for my trip to Europe. It was time for my second typhoid shot, so I located a public health office where they administered the necessary injection. This event used up the rest of my free time, and I had to rush to reach Manitou Springs in time for my ride up Pike's Peak.

The cog station held the train ready for its trip up the mountain. (Pike's Peak is so steep that a regular train does not have enough traction to pull the hill so this special train has cog wheels to enable it to make the journey.) The conveyance consisted of a single aluminum observation car with large Plexiglas windows and beautifully upholstered leather seats.

In 1890 when the route first opened, the locomotive was a steam engine. Today it is comprised of three 135-hp diesel power plants in tandem on the bed of the single locomotive. The track has an average grade of 17 % but in stretches, it reaches a pitch of 25 %, necessitating the powerful cog engine that now idled behind the observation car.

At 2:00 p.m. in the clear, cold air of 8,000 feet, we started our ascent of the mountain. We climbed up through the pine and quaking aspen forests. Three Alpine lakes that supply the City of Colorado Springs with crystalline water slid by our view. Upon reaching 12,000 feet, clouds began to sweep past our windows, obstructing our view for short periods. The elevation of our destination on top of the mountain was 14,110 feet. We were soon out of the train and walking over the rough rocky summit. The temperature was a brisk 30 degrees and, with a light snow falling, we all headed for the hot-coffee stand in one of the two buildings that crowned the mountain's peak. Our stay on the top lasted forty minutes.

Between the intermittent snow flurries, we had views of the vast mid-America plains rolling eastward. Soon we were in the warm confines of our Gray Line car, moving back down the narrow mountain road. Our driver told us that the past six consecutive years, the auto race to the Peak had been won by Maserati-type Indianapolis racecars. In fifteen minutes, we departed the barren waste of rocks, and reached timberline. Looking back on the ridge above us there stood six Big Horn Sheep in stark silhouette, outlined against the late afternoon sunset. The driver said that these were the first he had seen this fall, as they are very reclusive animals. With the passage of a few more minutes, the top of the mountain was lost in a heavy snowstorm. We arrived in Manitou Springs at 5:30, tired but exhilarated.

Pikes by Diverse Route

In the year 1806, Zebulon Pike had discovered and named the mountain. He failed in an attempt to climb the mountain and stated that it would *never* be scaled. So much for his prophesy of the future. Another interesting bit of history stated that the Paiute Indians brought their sick and aged and filled them with the strong mineral water from the local spring. They were convinced that the water had magical powers of healing.

About this time, a violent squall line crossed Colorado Springs with an accompanying electrical storm. Slashes of lightning flashed through the town as I returned to my third-floor room at the YMCA building. Claps of thunder shook the building while rain poured down in torrents. From my vantage point, I watched as people down in the streets ran for cover in the deluge. With each bolt of lightning, the night sky lit up with an iridescent yellow glow. The morning's paper had an article about a young lady who was struck and killed by lightning during the night. I felt fortunate to have completed my Pike's Peak trip and to have returned to my room before the wild storm arrived.

CHAPTER 9

October 8, 1947, Down the road again

On arising in the morning, I felt the effects of the previous day's typhoid shot. Sore and a little dizzy, I lay in bed an extra hour. Once I was up and moving about, the ill effect of the shot began to fade. The air was cool and crisp after the night's storm. I was picked up by a fellow en route to Pueblo. He was very entertaining, but I was afraid he was a bit of a smoke blower.

He said he was a personal friend of Joe E. Brown and was now returning from a trip to Los Angeles. He said that he traveled from quiz show to quiz show and had twenty-two thousand dollars in winnings from his recent trip. In my opinion, his story was most unlikely. As my Uncle Ralph used to say, "The world is full of bull; use your sifter!"

We drove south until we reached Pueblo. With my duffel bag on my shoulder, I walked a short distance until I was on the east side of town. Now my travels turned to the east as I stood on the edge of Route 50. In a few minutes, a seed salesman gave me a lift; and we were soon on our way to Dodge City, Kansas. Reaching the town of Las Animas, Colorado, we began to travel parallel to the Arkansas River. This area is steeped in the history of the old Santa Fe Trail. A hundred years ago, great ox carts would start out from Independence, Missouri, loaded with trade goods on their way to the Mexican southwest. These contraband traders of old followed the exact route we now traveled along the river. In those days, it was illegal for Americans to trade with the Mexicans; but the need was great and the business was lucrative.

Near the highway, we passed a huge oil, gas, and propane storage station that served a nearby oil field. My driver explained that there was only one large pipeline that led all the way back to Pueblo. The system used was to pump one item through, then inject a marker of colored dye material before sending the next item down the huge pipeline.

Late in the evening, our journey for the day ended in Dodge City. It is another location of historical interest. When the West was in its early prime, the railroad was built all the way to Dodge to take advantage of the beef trade. Great herds of cattle were driven north out of Texas on the Cimarron Trail that ended at the railhead. This system supplied the east coast of the United States with inexpensive meat.

This 318-mile day was the longest transit for a single day since leaving my home in Campbell. That evening I could not locate an inexpensive hotel so my benefactor of the day invited me to stay in his double room at the Lora Locke Hotel.

He was a congenial roommate, but he drank far too much for my likes. He offered me some booze, but when I declined, he did not try to influence me further. While he drank, he regaled me with stories of his childhood down in South Carolina.

One of his tales detailed fishing for crabs. The method was to take five or six cane poles, and place them in a line out into a shallow backwater pond. Once the poles were in place, he would tie a five-foot line to each pole with a piece of rotten fish at the end. He would wait a few minutes and then with net in hand, go from line to line. When he pulled each line up, an occasional crab would hang on until it broke the water's surface and then drop off into his net.

After he had completed several drinks, we went out to the famous Harvey House for dinner. This was an interesting restaurant as I had recently seen the movie, *The Harvey Girls*, that dealt with the history of the railroads and their introduction of this chain of fine eateries. The food was excellent and not too expensive. In a short time, we were back in our room. It became a long night as from across the room, a loud rumble of snores and incoherent mumbles came from my roommate.

In the morning, I was quick to pack and leave my friend who was still sleeping off his excess of alcohol.

CHAPTER 10

October 9, 1947, On to Kansas City, Missouri

I had a quick breakfast and was on the roadside by 8:00 a.m. A note here on a system that I had developed hitchhiking. In the morning at roadside, I would take out a piece of chalk and print in large letters on the side of my duffel bag a destination that would be one hundred to two hundred miles ahead. I discovered that if I wrote *New York City*, this seemed to put people off and they would not stop for someone traveling that far. This became another bit of hitchhiking psychology.

This day I had inscribed Kansas City on my bag upright in front of me. In a few minutes, I was picked up and was on the move eastward. At first, we passed through miles of wheat fields, but later we transited a corn belt. Mile after mile of shocked corn stacks were visible drying in the fields.

We passed through another rich field of oil wells. I observed hundreds of rocker arms pumping up and down, drawing wealth from beneath the earth. It made me wonder how many dirt-poor farmers had struck it rich and became millionaires almost overnight.

I arrived in Kansas City, Missouri, in the twilight of a beautiful fall day. Another banner day of 356 miles under my belt had been completed. The YMCA provided me with a room for one dollar fifty and a dinner of chicken potpie for an additional fifty cents. I decided that tomorrow I would take a break from my eastward trip to visit a girlfriend from high school days. Barbara Moore was an excellent student and her parents had sent her off to Cotty College, a finishing school in southwestern Missouri. A look at my map indicated a distance of less than 100 miles south would put me in her town.

Traveling south out of Kansas City took me past the farm of President Truman's brother. I stopped in Butler, Missouri, for lunch and arrived in the college town of Nevada by 2:00 p.m. I located a room in a hotel that was just a big house converted for roomers. A phone call to Barbara let me know that she would be out of her last class for the day by three. We met on the edge of a lovely lake on her campus.

We sat in the warm grass near the water's edge and talked of my doings since graduation from Campbell High School. Later, we walked up the hill to her red brick dormitory. I met her roommate from Iowa, and the three of us talked until it was time for Barb and me to walk into town for dinner. We located a wonderfully quaint restaurant that specialized in Kansas City steaks. The meal was superb, after all the cheap food I had eaten since departing California. All too soon, it was time to return her to the campus.

The reason for the early return provided a very humorous story: Seems that the college was very strict about their tender, young girls being back in their rooms no later than ten o'clock. One of the girls, being inventive, had a knotted rope that could be dropped out of a second story window for late arrivals. One of the instructors decided to climb up this rope to confront the girls. Unfortunately for him, they looked out and saw him coming and untied the rope.

The nosy instructor fell far enough to break his leg and the result was that for the rest of the semester, all the young ladies were required to be in the building no later than eight o'clock!

It seemed that I had just arrived when our time together was up. The interval had provided a wonderful interlude from the uncertainty of my day-to-day existence.

I returned to my room in the small village through the cool brisk air of an autumn night. The lovely sound of bells rang out from the tower of the city hall as I walked past in the eventide.

There was a short spell of homesickness in my remembrance of the bells of the congregational church of my hometown. But, in moments, the thought passed and the consideration of tomorrow's travels filled my thoughts.

CHAPTER 11

October 11-12, 1947,
Indianapolis motor speedway

Early in the morning, I ate breakfast at a greasy spoon. The drinking water was so full of chlorine that I decided it must be to cut the food grease.

I left town on Highway 54 in a Northwesterly direction toward St Louis. My first ride was with a pretty dance instructor. This marked the first time a single woman had picked me up since leaving California. We had a long discussion regarding the Negroes. This talk proved quite a shock to me as I had grown up in an area that had no blacks. The thrust of her tirade was that the "niggers were okay as long as they were kept on a level with farm animals." I think there is trouble brewing in this country with attitudes of this persuasion. This ride was of short duration, and I was soon out on the roadside again.

Another short ride followed. The driver was en route to Jefferson City, the capital of Missouri. He worked as a sociologist in the state prison in Jefferson City. We discussed the attitude of my previous driver, and he thought that a lot of the Black problems stem from this southern prejudice. He called her a cracker, a term that I had never heard before.

A lot of the sentiments flowed directly from the outcome of the Civil War, an event that was still alive in these parts. Often in the days ahead, I would ponder the positions of these two opinions that repeatedly boiled up in the southern United States.

The next ride took me all the way to St. Louis on the banks of the Mississippi River. The road that we drove passed through 200 miles of rolling, forested hills. This beautifully wooded country was broken with occasional small square fields hacked out of the thick green trees.

In these areas, the bright morning sun emphasized the gold color of the row on row of cornstalks ready for harvest. Later as we approached St. Louis, the air grew hazy from the smoke drift from the city's heavy industry.

On arrival in the city, I got out near a bus stop with my duffel bag on my shoulder. Before the bus arrived, another driver pulled over to give me a lift. He turned out to be a GI in the study of X-ray machines for the military. His hospital facility was close by, but he insisted on delivering me to the door of the local YMCA. On our way, we passed a big sign, **Budweiser Beer Co**. Under the emblem was written, "This is the largest brewery in the world".

The building covered four blocks and was seven stories high. I reached my destination; and after thanking him for his extra effort, hopped out in front of the YMCA. To my disappointment, there were no rooms available. On the clerk's suggestion, I walked a block to the Warwick Hotel and located a one-dollar room. My stay here was unremarkable, and I was up and on my way early the next morning.

The 7:00 a.m. air was filled with so much smoke that it was impossible to see the Mississippi down below as I crossed over the McArthur Bridge. My driver thought that the bridge had been recently renamed in honor of the recent World War II hero. A roadside sign stated "Land of Lincoln," and now the state of Illinois lay ahead. Without a stop, my ride transited the state. My benefactor was a young man on his way to Terre Haute, Indiana, to be married; and he was in a hurry!

We talked of what the transition from single to married life would be like, neither of us having any idea of what we were talking about.

Out of Terre Haute, I caught a ride in a hopped-up 'V-8 Ford roadster. This man had rebuilt this machine himself. He installed twin manifolds and a Columbia rear-end assembly. A long discussion of building and driving hot rods made the time pass quickly. We fairly howled across the miles until we arrived in Indianapolis.

I soon located the Young Men's Christian Association of Indianapolis. This provided me with night's lodging for one dollar. I ate a dinner of oysters and lettuce salad that was just excellent. Back in my room, I studied my maps; but in a short time, exhaustion overtook me, and sleep came with a rush. When I awoke the next morning, the room lights still burned and my clothes were still on. After taking a shower and changing my underwear and socks, I felt like a new man, ready to meet the day ahead. My plan was to travel out to the Indianapolis 500 motor speedway.

A short bus ride I was at the entrance to the track. This was the most famous auto racetrack in America. It was affectionately called the Brick Yard, from the bricks that form the roadbed. I had a special interest in the track because I had a friend who built racecars for the Indy 500. His name was Bob Allenger, and he lived near Campbell High School. I met him through my school project. During my three years at the shop, my interest was in the construction of a midget car. It had a Briggs and Strattan engine and a three-speed motorcycle transmission. It had a top speed in excess of fifty miles per hour. I was always trying to get it to go faster and someone recommended that the man to see was Allenger. We became friends, and I spent a lot of hours doing odd jobs in his shop, and he helped me improve my machine.

He built midgets for the California tracks, high-speed hydrofoils with P-38 engines for the Detroit Gold Cup races, and many cars for the Indy 500. Through him, I met several drivers for the 500; and from this opportunity, I developed a high interest in racing.

The day after my arrival, I met a watchman who, after some discussion, let me onto the track. The first thing I did was to walk the two-and-one-half-mile oval. I had heard several radio broadcasts of the event over the years. The opportunity to walk the track gave me a real feel of the various straightaways, infamous turns, and its brick surface. In one of the small buildings, a man was fine-tuning the suspension of his racer. He was familiar with my friend Allenger, and this provided the opportunity for a long discussion. Before departing, he gave me a brochure from the previous race.

CHAPTER 12

October 14-15, 1947, Across Ohio, West Virginia, and on to New Jersey

I started back on the road about noon headed for Columbus, Ohio, caught rides due east on Highway 40, and arrived in Columbus about 8:00 p.m.

Because of the time spent on the racetrack, the day's mileage was a short 174 miles. This evening, I decided to see a movie for a break in my routine. My finances were better than expected, so I decided on a night out. Next to the hotel where I was staying, the movie *Kitty* was playing and admission was twenty-five cents. This provided good entertainment for the evening.

There was nothing of interest to keep me in Columbus, so I was on the road early the next morning. With the word *Pittsburgh* chalked vertically on my duffel bag, I was fortunate in my first pickup. Yes, I had luck. The driver provided me with a lift straight through to Pittsburgh, Pennsylvania. My benefactor was the owner of a chain of forty-three restaurants. I listened for hours to his trials and tribulations of running such a large enterprise. Occasionally, I would make a comment, but mainly he wanted a mental backboard to bounce off his ideas. The miles rolled past and we soon crossed the little 25 mile northern tip of West Virginia. A short time passed, and we arrived in Pittsburgh in the early afternoon.

With daylight still bright, I discovered the Gulf Building. Its forty-three-story observation tower provided a bird's-eye view of the three rivers that make this town famous. Allegheny and Monongahela rivers join to create the Ohio, and all were visible from this high vantage point. It was interesting to see even in daylight the pronounced white glare that came from the many steel mills along the river. A man nearby explained that this glare came from the Bessemer Converters. These devices blow air through molten iron to remove the impurities in the steel-making process. This system also creates clouds of smog that envelop the nearby boroughs, or suburbs, as we would call them in California. I took a few photographs and then returned to the street.

I had the good fortune in meeting a knowledgeable young lady while I rode a tram in search of the Carnegie Institute. We were soon in conversation about the history of the city. After a long conversation, she invited me to come out to her parents' home to spend the night. Her folks lived in a palatial brick home on a hill overlooking the city. To reach the house, we took a small streetcar that climbed up a 45-degree slope. The views out the windows of this conveyance were spectacular.

She and her husband lived in a cottage on the rear of the property. The parents took me in with great hospitality. What a treat to have a home-cooked dinner after the days I had spent on the road. The mother, father, and three other sisters made the evening warm and homelike. Later that evening, the girl I had met and her husband took me out in their car to see the city by night. Once again, the most notable view was of the Bessemer Converters now glowing red along the river in the dark night. This place was considered Steel Town USA. After an hour's drive, we returned to her folks' home. I went up to my room and found a small radio at the bedside. The radio in itself was a small item but what an enjoyment after austere cheap hotel rooms.

I was up at eight and enjoyed a fine meal of French toast and sausage, and then, with many thanks for their hospitality, I departed for the city area. The town health department provided me with a typhoid shot for my schedule of necessary inoculations for my intended travel to Europe.

I departed Pittsburgh after lunch and was at the entrance of the Pennsylvania Turnpike by twelve thirty. Luck deserted me and I stood stranded at roadside until four thirty. After the long wait the driver who picked me up turned out to be very interesting. He made his living driving midget racecars. We had a long talk about the Indianapolis 500 and other racing events.

The turnpike was originally a railroad bed that was later converted to a high-speed highway. There were seven tunnels that allow for a straight drive through mountains and on eastward across the country. A patchwork of small farms and rolling hills framed this magnificent highway. The speed limit must have been very fast as all the traffic fairly flew.

I arrived in Breezewood, Pennsylvania, at sunset. I was able to find lodging in the Maple Lawn Inn for the night. The owners were an elderly couple that went out of their way to be hospitable to me. A clean, homelike room for two dollars complete with a hot home-cooked meal made the day.

In the early morning when I arose, a thick fog pressed against the windowpanes of my room. I took my time showering and going over the articles in my duffel bag. It is interesting how much thought can be put into reviewing one's articles when there are only a few. Even a length of string and a pair of safety pins were carefully stored in their special place.

I walked to the turnpike at 9:00 a.m. and was soon picked up by a Ford delivery truck that rolled to a stop out of the dense fog. We traveled only a few minutes before we broke out into the dazzling sunshine. The gorgeous colors of Indian summer appeared all around us. What an amazing array of beauty filled the roadside! They ran a range of hues from greens, dark browns, bright reds, and on to brilliant yellows. My grandfather would have had a field day with his paints and easel in this magnificent setting.

Late in the day, I caught a ride on to Jersey City, New Jersey. This gentleman was driving a brand new Dodge delivery truck while towing another one behind. When we arrived at a storage yard in Jersey, I helped him remove the clearance lights and vacuum brakes on the trailing truck. As the night before a thick fog closed in around us. I was glad to have his company as we passed through an old residential area. We were under the gaze of gangs of boys that roamed the streets as we walked along. My partner carried the parts from the towing kit while I carried my duffel bag on one shoulder and held a tire iron and a nut wrench in my free hand. One of these gangs was composed of kids not more than eleven or twelve. What were they doing out wandering about at this hour of the night? The group that worried me consisted of seven boys who could easily have been in their twenties.

They followed us for a block before disappearing into the fog that swirled about the street lamps. Up ahead I spotted a sign that stated Travelers Tourist Home. We went in and I secured a room for the night. My companion called for a cab to take him to his hotel in Manhattan. My room was a walk-up, three stories to a bed under the slanting eves. I located a hamburger joint a block away for dinner. While walking to and from this eatery, I had eyes in the back of my head looking for the wandering gangs of kids but was happy to see not another person. Returning to my room, I looked over the card the lady had given me on my first arrival.

The card read:

20 minutes to Times Square Radio City
First-class rooms at moderate rates
fare to New York 10 cents
Mrs. T. Beyer, 70 Van Reipen Avenue, Jersey City 6, NJ

The following morning after breakfast, I rode a subway over to New York City. I had crossed the continent for less than fifty dollars.

CHAPTER 13

October 17-24, 1947,

New York City sightseeing

On my arrival from Jersey I traveled by subway to downtown Manhattan. In a few minutes, I located a room at the Sloan House YMCA located about one-half block from the famous New Yorker Hotel. Once settled in my room I took some of my clothes down to be cleaned and pressed. While this was in progress, I took a nap until 6:00 p.m.

Once I had retrieved my clothes, I located an unusual place for dinner. The place was called Horn and Hardits Automat and had a wall covered with small square doors. Behind each glass door could be seen a different food. After making a choice, I inserted a coin and as the door popped open, I had my selected food.

On the opposite sidewall, there were small two-person tables that provided a place to eat. It intrigued me, as I had never seen anything like this in California. Completing my meal, I walked to the Empire State Building.

The price of a ride to the top of the Empire State Building was a dime, and I soon was on the observation deck high over the city. When I first arrived, the visibility was only one mile but soon it cleared to three. What a view! In one direction, the Time Square area called the Great White Way was visible with its white and colored lights of all varieties.

Down in the dock area I could see the ocean liner *Queen Mary* in a great blaze of lights. The guard said she was to have sailed at 7:00 p.m. but now at eight-thirty she was still at her moorings. This was of special interest to me as my aunt, Helen Sturges, was a passenger on board returning to her home in England.

What a coincidence; I thought I would arrive in New York City too late to wish her bon voyage. She had been visiting my mother in California the past month before I departed on my trip. While I hitchhiked across the country, she had zipped across the nation by streamlined train.

Interesting views of the dark East River and the Hudson could be seen from this eagle's aerie. Twinkling lights showed the path of ships and ferries underway over the black surface of water. In another direction, I could see the lighted torch of the Statue of Liberty guarding the entrance to New York Harbor. It was getting cold, and I returned to the elevator for my descent to the street below.

The next day, I ate lunch uptown and then took a ferry out to the Statue of Liberty. What a sight to see the lady take shape out of the fog as we approached Bedloe's Island where she stands. The salt-sea air has oxidized the copper statue to a soft metallic green hue. Inside the door in her base, we tourists started climbing the two hundred steps that took up into the cap that crowns her head. Here we discovered small windows that allowed a view out into the harbor. A short distance away, we caught a glimpse of Ellis Island, where thousands and thousands of immigrants entered America. The door up the stairs into the torch was locked so that ended the climb upward. Once again, down below, a fifteen-minute ferry ride returned me to Manhattan.

I have a cousin, Barbara Cutting Halpern, who was completing her internship as a doctor in a local hospital. It was still early enough, and I decided to find my way to her apartment at 515 West 122nd St., Manhattan.

Consulting my address book, I rode a subway to her area. Then I walked four blocks through an unlighted Negro area, and I arrived at the apartment of her and her husband.

Unfortunately, no one was home, and I was surprised to discover that her neighbors on both adjoining apartments do not know who they are. In the small town of Campbell where I grew up, everyone knows all the people that are near neighbors and all the shopkeepers on the main street. This lack of knowledge of one's close inhabitants is incomprehensible to me. Just another fact of big-city life I was forced to realize.

On the return trip to the YMCA, I spent my time watching the characters on the subway. Several seem to spend time mumbling to themselves. From the perspective of a country boy, they seem nervous and preoccupied with their own problems as opposed to the friendly, outgoing Westerners that I have grown up with.

The following morning, I had my breakfast in the Y cafeteria and decided on a tour of the Rockefeller Center not far away. A short walk in the morning sunshine took me to the headquarters of the center. I purchased a ticket that stated, "Guest of ROCKEFELLER CENTER-GUIDED TOUR." The guide is a good-humored young lady.

The center belongs to Columbia University and was leased to Mr. Rockefeller until the year A.D 2014. The twelve acres were built between 1931-1939 and is composed of several unique buildings. RCA., English, and French buildings plus the entertainment building are all of modern architecture. As an example, the French building is faced with French marble while the elevators are lined with mahogany from French Africa.

In the entrance to one of the foyers, there was a mural depicting the great classes that have made America. The workers are on one side, and the thinkers on the other. Another mural that was unique appeared on the ceiling. It was of three great men standing atop pillars. What made it unusual was that they all appeared to lean in your direction and gaze down upon you. As you moved to the other side of the room, they seemed to turn and continue to stare down on you. This painting is a wonderful feat of optical allusion.

Next, we walked over to the RCA Building and rode the elevator up to the seventieth-floor observation platform. There, to my surprise, I saw that the *Queen Mary* was still alongside the dock. I decided to rush down and try to catch my aunt Helen before she sailed. Too late, the tugs were pushing the great ship out into the channel as I arrived at the dockside. What a sight to see! Her two red funnels giving off a light smoke, as the world's largest ship afloat made ready for sea.

After lunch, I decided to take a tour of the bowery and Chinatown. In the days of the Dutch ownership of New York, the bowery was out in the country from the city. The tour guide pointed out a tree that was prominent in the book *A Tree Grows in Brooklyn*. The area was home to bums and winos who lay in all the doorways and alleys.

We climbed down the steps into a church that had once been an opium den. Now it serves as a place where the down and out sleep and are fed decent meals. The preacher was an interesting fellow who had traveled the world over before joining the ministry and devoting his life to the care of these needy people.

Our next stop was Chinatown, where we walked through the largest diamond center in the world. From the outside, this place looked like an ordinary store. Once inside, we saw that it was heavily guarded. Many plainclothes men, whose coats bulged with side arms, stood in alcoves throughout the building. Someone in our group gave a sudden slap of his hands, and several of these plain clothes men gave an involuntary jump. One of the store managers was not amused, and this prompted a stern lecture to our party.

Back on the street, I had a hard time comprehending the large numbers of low-life men lying around the area. With my small-town background, this was unfathomable. Back home, the few drunks in our town were kept in their homes, out of public view. I suppose the end of the World War has created a lot of unemployment, with its physical and mental disruption of these men. It provided me with a very depressing view of mankind. I concluded it was a huge problem that needed to be solved by the city fathers of New York City.

The following morning I took a tour of the NBC building. The opportunity to sit in the broadcasting booth and listen to H. V. Kaltenborn gave his news program, was an interesting opportunity.

Next, we went into a room where they produced sound effects. Examples were the sound of rain provided by birdseed falling on paper to make the sound of rain; while squeezing a hot bottle full of sand gave off the sound of a man walking through snow.

In another room, we were shown a model of the broadcasting chambers. These were unique in that they were rooms cushioned within larger rooms in an attempt to screen out the vibrations of the subway that rumbled beneath the building.

Next, we were given a demonstration of television. A few members of our tour group went into another room and stood before the camera and talked to the rest of our group. In our room, we could hear and see them in action. I thought this medium would make a big impact on the future of communication. The tour concluded with our watching the rehearsal of the "The Hour of American Music".

I walked up Wall Street and entered the New York Stock Exchange. Looking down from above, I observed it appeared to be bedlam. Men with different-colored coats ran this way and that, shouting to other people who stood in small booths, taking orders for blocks of stock. Paper slips were strewn all over the floor of the great hall. I was told that it cost between fifteen thousand dollars and twenty thousand dollars to purchase a seat on the exchange.

Out on the street I walked up a short distance and came upon a graveyard and an old church. On further investigation, it proved to be the church that George Washington had used in 1776 during the revolutionary days of our country. The graveyard had several historical graves of early Americans.

While walking, I met two interesting men also studying the gravestones. One was a young man from Prague, Czechoslovakia, who was touring the United States, lecturing in universities on seven European governments.

His companion was a man from Norway on his way to New Orleans to study the production of oleomargarine. The one from Prague gave me several addresses of inexpensive places for students to stay in Poland and Czechoslovakia. We sat on the steps of the church and talked for an hour on life in America in contrast to their countries.

October 20, and it was time to stop touring and start a serious search for a job on a ship bound for Europe. I went to at least fifteen shipping companies and the answer was always the same: "You must first join the seaman's union."

I was becoming discouraged after hours of tramping the streets of Manhattan. I decided to go to the seaman's union hall and find out what was necessary to become a member. It was a fruitless trip as I was told there were no openings in the union. I was also told I was too young and furthermore, "get the hell out of here and stop wasting our time!" The day was not very productive, and I decided to return to my room in the Y and think of other possibilities.

That evening, I met a young man named Ted Overstreet in the Y dining room. He was a Canadian navy sailor on leave. The next day, we decided to join forces and take a tour on a sightseeing boat around the island of Manhattan.

On this trip, we met two tourist girls from Detroit, Michigan. We took them out to Coney Island and walked around in the dark. It was late in the season and the place was boarded up for the winter.

The girls had reservations to a play for the evening so we rode the subway back to town. Ted and I made plans to meet them after the play at the Hotel Astor where they were staying. The two of us returned to the Sloan House YMCA for dinner. Later we met down in the lobby and traded stories for two hours while we waited for the girls to return from their play.

When we picked them up, they had not eaten so we took them to a hamburger joint for some food. While they ate, we talked, and I drank a coke. Suddenly, I was seized with a terrible pain in my left side and groin. Sweat popped out all over my body, and I was so dizzy that I could not stand up straight. I thought for sure I had appendicitis, and we had to leave the girls in a hurry.

We returned to the Y, but the house doctor had gone home for the night. The desk clerk suggested that we go over to the French hospital nearby. Before we arrived, I vomited a couple of times and was in a great state of anxiety. In the hospital, two young doctors asked a lot of questions and gave a careful examination. The diagnosis was a kidney stone. They said, "Drink a lot of fluids, and it will pass in a day or two".

They then sent me on my way—without a bill! I returned to my room in the Y and lay down alone and in abject misery. Luck came to my aid during the night. I passed the stone and after a long sleep, I was once again in good health. The following morning I met Ted down in the breakfast room, and he was amazed at my full recovery. I thanked him for his support the night before, and we set out on another day of city exploration.

CHAPTER 14

Lesson learned

We set out to find the girls at the Hotel Astor. On our way there, we went down into a subway to catch a train in their direction. In the city of New York, there were a lot of nefarious con men ready to prey on bumpkins that were the likes of us. If you are from out of town, it is evident to these crooks by your dress and your habit of looking up at tall building as you walk along the avenues. I'm sure there are many other clues obvious to them.

As we stood in the semidarkness down in the tunnel waiting for our train, a man approached us. He was short, swarthy, with greasy hair and sweat-stained face. In a minute, he produced a ring and a watch from his pocket. While he accomplished this, he continued to look around and over his shoulder, with a look of fright on his face. He informed us that these items were very valuable and that he was in dire need of money for his sick child.

We were not that gullible, but in all of us, there's a bit of larceny until we learn from bitter experience that honesty is the best path in life. *Ah, we thought these items are probably hot but valuable.* He started with a high price on the diamond ring and the Bulova watch, but with the thought that we held the upper hand, we bartered him down and down. All the time the negotiations were in progress he kept on with his whiny voice while constantly looking nervously this way and that. In the end, I bought the ring for twelve dollars, and Ted bought the watch for ten. What a steal!

Before we could turn around, the little man had disappeared in the crowd. Now panic set in as we realized that we probably had some valuable, stolen articles. Off we went on the first train that stopped in our location. Two stops later we jumped off the train just as it was about to pull out of the station and ran to get on another one going in the opposite direction. All the time we continued to scan the crowds to see if we were being followed. Up out of the subway we climbed on a city bus only to change a few blocks later to another one. Now we began to calm down and consider our condition.

It was time to determine what a haul we had made on this transaction. Down in the side streets, we looked for a small jewelry store. Full of fright at the possibility of being apprehended, we at last built up our nerve and entered a small one-man store to have our merchandise appraised.

The old gentleman behind the counter looked us over for several seconds before taking our items for inspection. He placed his jeweler's glass in one eye and spent a few moments inspecting my ring and then pried the lid off the back of Ted's watch to study it carefully.

Without a word, he looked at us for a few more moments before asking in a solemn foreign accent, "And where did you boys get these articles?"

The urge to break and run was almost overwhelming, but we stammered that someone had given them to us. With that, he handed back the items to us and said, "The ring is glass set in brass—don't wear it as it will turn your finger green."

To Ted he added, "The watch has a Bulova face, but inside it has Mickey Mouse works; I hope you young men realize you have been bilked. Let it be a lesson that you can't get something for nothing."

Much chagrined, we left the shop and considered what to do next. Later, we decided to have a bit of fun with my new purchase. We took the subway to the Grand Central Station and entered the great waiting room and found a seat on an empty bench. I walked about fifteen feet and lay my ring down on the marble floor and then returned to my seat. The results were hilarious; in a few moments, a man came along toting a heavy suitcase and when he spied the ring, he stopped.

He looked furtively this way and that before bending quickly over to scoop up the ring. With perfect timing, I called out in a loud voice, "Is that your property?" He shot straight up and strode off in a hurry. We sat and rolled with laughter. After three runs with this game, we let a prim-looking young woman pick up the ring and go unmolested. She disappeared down the strand, still holding the ring up against the light, turning it this way and that, admiring her lucky find.

CHAPTER 15

Time from New York City to Baltimore by bus

It was time to stop sightseeing and get on with my job search. After failure to locate work with three more steamship companies, I thought of another idea.

I searched out an office that was involved with the Marshall Plan. Their function was to organize the shipping of relief material to Europe. Once again, I scored a strikeout for a job, but a secretary suggested that I go down to Baltimore where a lot of foreign ships depart to cross the Atlantic.

Another reason for a trip to Baltimore was that I carried a letter of introduction to the shipping firm of Dickman, Wright, & Pugh. My uncle, Cap Williams, sailed as a ship's captain for this firm during WW II.

He gave me the name of a man to locate in this company that he thought might be able to assist me in my search for work.

It was time to try a new venue. On October the 24, 1947, I rose early, showered, packed my duffel bag, and bought a bus ticket to Baltimore.

My friend Ted had to go over to New Jersey to see relatives, so he joined me on the first leg of my journey. We missed two busses before we departed New York City at noon for my trip south. We parted company in the bus terminal in Jersey City, and I was once again on my own.

My seatmate on the trip south was a young lady who was en route to Miami, Florida, to be married. We had a long and interesting discussion about expectations of her new life with her GI fiancé.

It was 11:30 p.m. when my bus arrived in a rundown bus station in Baltimore. In a tired state, I wandered about until I found a cheap bum hotel. My two-and-half-dollar room was dirty, and the walls had holes bored through from previous occupants looking for excitement. The room had two single beds, one on each wall. I was soon sound asleep in one of them. During the night, without my knowledge, another renter came into the room and occupied the other bunk.

Around 2:00 or 2:30 a.m., there was a loud crash, and the door flew open. In rushed two cops with powerful flashlights, and guns drawn. They hosed the two of us down with their lights. First me and then across the room to the other occupant which brought my first realization that there was another person in the room. They rushed over, and one policeman grabbed the young man by his unkempt stringy hair and jerked him out of bed onto the floor.

He cried out in alarm; and in his struggles, a pistol flew out of his bed and clattered to the floor. While one cop handcuffed the boy, the other officer gathered up the gun. A moment later, they departed without a word to me. To manage my fright, I turned on the room light and sat on the edge of my bed. It took only a moment for me to reach the realization that sleep would be impossible. I dressed and repacked my duffel bag and walked out into the misty rain that filled the dark of night.

The bus station was a short walk, and I was soon seated on a dirty splintered bench in front of the ticket booth. The silent attendant watched me but said nothing as I dozed until daybreak. In the light of day, I received instructions on the location of a YMCA. The room I rented was clean and without holes in the wall. I slept until nine then showered, shaved, and made my way to the shipping offices of Dickman, Wright, & Pugh. They read the letter of introduction from my uncle and then sent me to a government building to procure my seaman's papers.

CHAPTER 16

Bureaucratic battle

In an initial interview, I was informed that being under age eighteen, it would be necessary to get written permission from my mother to obtain seaman's papers. I called my mother at my stepfather's home and asked her to send the necessary permission by express mail.

This cost my pocketbook four dollars and eighty cents, which seemed excessive; but there was no alternative. Unable to do anything until I received the permission, I decided to take the time to go to Washington D.C. This plan also failed as I got soaked in a downpour of rain while trying to hitchhike out of town. I returned to the Y, washed out my clothes in the room sink, wrote letters, and read. Later, I paid a nickel for a pass that allowed me to ride all over town on the streetcar system. The rest of the afternoon was spent sightseeing the area from the tram.

There were three boys quartered in my present room in the YMCA. One just mustered out of the Navy and had started a job with General Electric. He and I took an instant like to each other so we often went out to eat our meals together. The other fellow—I was afraid—was a bad actor. He went out in the evenings with a pistol to hold up homosexuals. Late at night, he returned to our room with a friend who shared his bed? He is a strange, mentally sick fellow that I watched and avoided.

The GE boy and I took our valuables and deposited them in the front desk safe for more security. In addition, I took the precaution of writing a description of this felon and his activities. I included this information with my valuables in the safe, in the event anything happened to me.

Two days later, a letter arrived from California with the necessary written permit from my mother. The following morning I was in the government offices joining a long line, to be interviewed. Three hours later, it was my turn to talk to the officials. Only then did I discover that my wait had been in vain as this was not the proper line.

It was three fifty on a Friday afternoon before I finally was granted my interview. I was then informed it would be necessary to obtain four photos, my social security card, and my passport before moving forward in the process. Bureaucratic obstruction rather than information seemed to characterize the day. Nothing more could be done until Monday morning, and this delay provided me with another free weekend.

The evening was warm as I walked around Baltimore, talking to people on the street. One point of interest was the three blocks of open-produce market. One of the characters that I met here was a young black boy of eight, shelling lima beans. He was proud of his two-dollar pay for an eight-hour day.

We talked while he worked, discussing the America that he had never seen outside the limits of Baltimore.

This evening, the YMCA was throwing a dance; and I met a young sailor who just returned from England, and the two of us went in search of women.

I met a nice young girl named Onea Astor, and my navy friend found another young lady. The four of us had a wonderful evening of dancing and chatting. We took the girls home to Queens on the subway. The following morning, I met Onea for an early morning Methodist Church service. After church, her parents served us a wonderful brunch and after many thanks, I departed with the intention to return one day.

With the afternoon free, I boarded a bus for Washington D.C. to see the sights of the nation's capital. I hiked the broad steps up to the Capitol, climbed the Washington monument, and then toured the Archives building.

There was so much to see and do in our nation's capital that an afternoon is only a teaser. Exhausted, I rode a bus back to Baltimore in the evening. I slept most of the return bus trip and went straight to bed on reaching the YMCA.

Monday morning and it was time to obtain my seaman's papers. I returned to the government offices with the necessary documents in hand and after another long wait, I received my U.S. Merchant Mariner's Document. I have spent a week working my way through the web of bureaucratic red tape!

With my seaman's papers in hand, I returned to Dickman, Wright, & Pugh; and they, in turn, provided me with a letter of introduction, and sent me off to the Seaman's Union Hall. The man that I spoke to after a long wait was the union steward. My first impression of him was not very complimentary. He was overweight, with food stains all over the front of his dirty wrinkled shirt, and he spoke like an uneducated bum who was now the cock of the roost. He acted as if he was doing me a real favor just to talk to me.

I was in for a shock. I discovered that to join *his* union there would be a fee of four hundred dollars. This was then the size of my bankroll, and, therefore, it was not an option. Next, I was informed that there was no way to depart a United States ship in a foreign port without being required to return on the same ship. (This was a law put into effect in the 1920s to strengthen the seaman's union.)

That information provided the final blow. I thanked him for his time and departed in a discouraged state. On my way out, I talked to an old sailor who was sitting in the rear of the hiring hall, and he filled me in with worthwhile information.

He told me that if you jump ship in a foreign port, no one will chase you; but, of course, you can't get your passport and visa properly stamped. This fellow said that I should try to get on a foreign ship as a replacement for a missing crew member.

The pay would be next to nothing, but there would be no union dues, and I would be allowed to check into the country of arrival with my passport as a visitor. This, I thought, would provide me with a method of working my way overseas. Encouraged with this information, I returned to my room with high expectations for tomorrow.

The next day was typical of several to follow. Early breakfast followed with a bus ride down to the dock area to search for employment opportunities. One day I went to nine foreign shipping offices. On another day made the disappointing discovery that I had missed a trip to Ireland by two hours. I located a total of two leads that might be available in ten or twelve days.

Each day that passed cost more money out of my meager supply, and the dread of failure loomed more likely.

Aerial View of Harbor showing Fort McHenry

To break the discouragement, I decided to take a day off. A streetcar took me down to Fort McHenry, and I read the account of Francis Scott Key writing "The Star-Spangled Banner." I spent a couple of hours hiking around, investigating the battlements, and reading the historical information.

That evening after dinner, I was idly reviewing my options when I remembered having written a letter the previous year. The weekly magazine Look wrote an article about the American Friends Service Committee and their work in sending relief livestock to countries devastated in WW II. The article ended with an address in New Windsor, Maryland. Young people could apply for a job to become a shipboard cattle tender to Europe. I had written at age sixteen but never received a reply and so, had forgotten the event until now. I proceeded to dig a road map out of my duffel bag and discovered that New Windsor was only a short distance from my present location. I decided that tomorrow, I would hitchhike to New Windsor and check it out.

CHAPTER 17

New Windsor, Maryland

I was up at six, ate breakfast, and proceeded to check out of the Baltimore YMCA. Travelling the road, through picturesque villages and rolling hills, it took me until noon to reach New Windsor. The town is small—perhaps there were five hundred people all in all. I made a few inquires, and I soon located what in previous times had been known as Blue Ridge College and now housed the relief center.

Upon entering the main office, I noticed there was only one small elderly man on duty. I introduced myself to one Benjamin Bushong, executive secretary of The Heifer Project Committee. It took only a few minutes to explain my interest and note that I had written to this address the previous year. Mr. Bushong stood up and went over to a dust-covered file cabinet and, after a few moments of rummaging, returned with my application of the previous year. He interviewed me for another half hour before offering me a job in their workshops. The pay would be fifty cents an hour plus board and room. Overtime would be one dollar and twelve cents per hour. I would be eligible to work on the first ship traveling to Europe.

My luck had now changed dramatically. Not only did I have a job but also a place to stay out of the miserable frontal weather that swept down upon us. The temperature dropped rapidly while outside the wind howled, and heavy rain and hail pelted the countryside with the arrival of a nor'easter. Had I been two hours late leaving Baltimore, I would have been caught outside in this foul storm.

One of the young men who worked here arrived to deliver me over to the living quarters. In a few minutes, I was assigned a bed and a locker to store my few articles. In the few hours before supper, there was time to acquaint myself with the plant layout of the relief center. My crude map showed the general scheme of the relief center.

RELIEF CENTER, NEW WINDSOR, MARYLAND, 1947

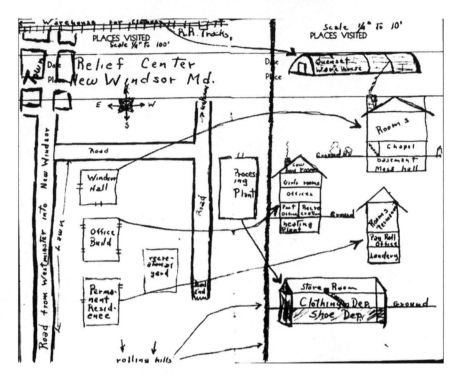

November 5, 1947

I started first day of work at 8:00 a.m. I was sent to the shoe-packaging department where pairs of used shoes were loaded into fifty-pound bundles. The work was terribly boring. The saving grace was the girl who worked with me on the line. She was eighteen, pretty, and great fun to banter with.

Before the lunch break, I heard that there was an opening in the transportation department for a driver's helper. I went over during the lunch hour and was hired on the spot. Fortunately, I had my California truck driver's license. I was given the remainder of the afternoon off and, with the clearing weather, took a long walk out into the surrounding countryside.

November 6, 1947

I did not have to report for work until noon, so I walked into town and paid for a badly needed haircut. The barber was an interesting fellow whose family had lived in the area since before the Civil War. He had lots of stories about local history. Later, with completion of lunch, I reported to the transportation shed and helped load two trucks with outgoing relief supplies before supper.

November 7, 1947

I rolled out of my bunk at 5:00 a.m. and reported for my first day on the road. The driver and I checked out the big Federal semi that would be our rig for the day. Our run took us to Richmond, Virginia, via Washington and Bowling Green.

Completing a day of loading and unloading our truck, we pulled back into the center about 2:00 a.m., Saturday morning.

Saturday, November 8, 1947

I met my driver at 9:00 a.m. First, we unloaded the truck that we had delivered the night before and then reloaded it with new supplies for the docks in New York. We completed our work in the afternoon and now had the next two days off. After a quick shower and shave, I boarded a bus for Baltimore to meet a girl for a dance at the YMCA. The evening was a lot of fun until 1:00 a.m. when it was time to locate a room for the night. This endeavor was an absolute failure.

The Navy football team was in town for a big game and this, coupled with the horse-racing season, had filled all the available rooms for rent. My next effort was to go to the Greyhound bus station to buy a ticket back to New Windsor. Although a Greyhound bus passed through New Windsor, their franchise did not allow the drop-off of passengers in that town. I located another bus company on the far side of Baltimore that served the nearby town of Westminster in the middle of the night. One tired boy checked in to a hotel room in Westminster about 4:00 a.m. (I did not return to the center because they have a lockdown at 11:00 p.m.)

November 9, 1947

Enjoyed a nine-o'clock breakfast and then made my way back to the center in New Windsor. That night's trip had a 10:00 p.m. report time so I had the rest of the day free of duty. I decided to take a long hike through the countryside. The blue sky was clear but there was an icy wind blowing that made me walk fast to stay warm.

The landscape was beautifully carpeted with green after the recent rains. The trees had all "turned" with the approach of winter and so the combination of colors made a beautiful picture for the mind to file away. After the hike, I returned to my room for a nap, in preparation for our night departure. We had the big red Federal truck inspected and was on the roll for New York City by ten o'clock.

November 10, 1947

We pulled into Jersey City, New Jersey, with the first shafts of morning light. Our destination is pier 9, which is located directly over the Holland Tunnel. In a short time, we off-loaded our bales of relief clothing destined for Europe. We drove a short distance into New York City for a load of empty boxes to deliver to New Windsor. A short stop for a meal and we were headed south for home. Twenty-two hours later, we pulled into the center, our day's work complete.

During the next two weeks, I made trips to New York City and several down into Pennsylvania. In one week, my pay slip showed ninety hours. My trip diary entries were never made as I was in a fog of fatigue.

Sunday, November 16, 1947

Having a day off, I hitchhiked up to Gettysburg. Saw many lighted maps of those historic days of the 1860s. Toured the Jenny Wade House, looked at many historic homes with bullet scars still visible. Walked through the famous wheat field that was taken, lost, and retaken so many times that it would have been possible,—the guide informed us—to walk across a solid mass of the fallen. Another location of interest to me was a spring where men from the opposing sides came in the night to refill their canteens and talk to their daytime mortal enemies. I felt that every American should come and experience this historic ground.

December 1, 1947

In the last twenty-two hours, I had completed my last trip in the old Federal semi. Over the last weeks, I had driven more and more until we were now splitting the behind the wheel driving time fifty-fifty.

It was on my last trip that I nearly came to grief. The time is 3:00 a.m., and I am passing three trucks that were stopped at signal light. The green light came on as I came up from behind them and I pulled out to pass as they were slow in getting underway. Hidden from my view by these trucks was a sign that stated, "Road under repair ahead—two lanes reduced to one." I was well committed to pass the other trucks when, suddenly, there was a heavy-timbered roadblock in front of me. There was no way that I could stop in the remaining distance, so I downshifted one gear and wound the engine up into the red line while accelerating. At the last possible moment before hitting the barrier, I cut back into the open lane.

The trailer heeled far over and the tires howled, but I squeaked through with a big load of luck. My partner congratulated me on pulling it off, but it was a long time before my heart stopped racing. Thus ended my last day of work with the service center transportation department.

I had been informed the previous week that I was assigned as cattle tender on an Italian vessel sailing for Italy in ten days.

It was time to prepare for my trip to Europe. The first item that requires attention is a trip to Washington D.C. to obtain visas for Italy and France. (Before leaving California, I had already obtained a visa for England.)

The trip into Washington DC was uneventful until I went into the French Embassy. They looked at my passport. "You are only seventeen and will be traveling alone? No, we will not issue you a visa!" After several minutes of argument, they agreed that if I could get the Italians to give me a visa, they would do the same. I went directly to the Italian Embassy and they gave me the same response: "No!"

I was frustrated until I came up with an idea. After the official went back into his office, I talked to the young lady secretary who worked behind the desk. It was a few minutes before lunch hour so I asked her if I could buy her a sandwich and ask her advice on how to obtain my visa. To my great relief, she agreed to go out with me.

We talked during the meal and I told her of my desire to get to Europe. My story must have been convincing because she suggested that if I would leave my passport with her she would see what she could do. I was to return in two days and see if she was successful. In two days time, I returned and, true to her word, my Italian visa was neatly stamped into my passport. The lady's name was Ines Ghiron, a thirty-one-year-old Italian girl working in the Italian Embassy in Washington DC.

My next stop was the French Embassy, and I located the fellow who had said that if I could obtain an Italian visa, he would do the same with the French. This ploy went through without trouble, and so I went back to New Windsor, Maryland, with the necessary paperwork in hand.

It was now time to make my final preparations for my voyage across the Atlantic. I bought a few extra pairs of socks, work pants, and underwear. However, the most important items purchased were heavy, waterproof jacket and a woolen watch cap. Someone who had been on a previous trip told me that the food would be almost totally starch, and so I went out to buy a small box of oranges. Unable to find oranges, I settled for a half box of lemons; and this would have interesting consequences in the days ahead.

Another item that I went out to buy was a carton of cigarettes. I am not a smoker but had been told that of all small items, the cigarette was, by far, the most valuable item to use in barter. A stash of twenty-five one-dollar bills completed my additions for the trip.

CHAPTER 18

The Heifer Project Committee

The Heifer Project is a program sponsored by the Brethren Service Committee, is an offshoot of the Quakers. They supplied and sent cattle to Europe in parallel with the United States' Marshall Plan. Southern Europe had been stripped of cattle. During WW II, soldiers shot anything that moved. Civilians ate the remainder to survive during the terrible upheaval caused by the great army battles on the Italian Peninsula during World War II.

Now the farmers were destitute, and these cows were a gift from the American people. The hope was that this effort will return local farmers to milk and beef production.

Cows were gathered from all parts of the United States and shipped to the Baltimore docks for embarkation. Next, church officials designated the cattle to a specific ship for transportation to Europe. Men were assigned as cattle tenders to board ship along with the livestock.

Five a.m., December 3, 1947: Six of us, cattle tenders, departed New Windsor, Maryland, in the early morning for transportation to the Baltimore docks. The station-wagon ride to Pier 8, Locust Point, Baltimore Harbor, was uneventful. We were all filled with anticipation wondering what will happen next. The ship we were assigned to was called the *Humanitos* (Italian for "mankind"). I was shocked to see a rundown rust bucket that would be a perfect fit for a Jack-London sea story. This ship was originally a Liberty ship named the *Claus Spreckles*. At the conclusion of WW II, she was sold to the Italians. Her profile was a solid sheet of rust with traces of black and gray paint smeared here and there. Today her Plimsoll line was below the water line halfway toward the stern of the ship. (This indicated she was not properly load balanced.) Her principal mission was the transportation of coal from the United States to Italy. Today, she had, in addition to her overload of coal, stalls for one hundred sixty head of cattle on the top deck yet to be swung aboard.

Six cattle tenders are all smiles. The author is fourth from the left.

This day was one of pandemonium as we, six American cattle tenders, met the Italian crew. We made a quick trip to locate our quarters and unloaded our few personal items and then hustled back on deck to go to work.

Stevedores were in a flurry of activity as they loaded feed, composed of tons of hay and grain, on top of the deck hatch covers. Into this mix of activity, one hundred sixty bawling cattle were landed willy-nilly amidst the cluttered deck.

These pregnant heifers had been bred so that they will produce calves a short time after their arrival in Italy. Timing was the key and was based on a trip of ten days to cross the Atlantic from Baltimore to Italy. However, due to shipping delays and other factors, a few of the cattle were already delivering their offspring as they boarded the ship. What a mess! What an introduction to the life of a cattle tender.

As the cattle are swung aboard ship, we were directed to move them into their stalls. It was hectic and very funny, as three of us had no experience with moving pregnant cows. In the beginning, we jumped about with the hope of escaping the kicks of the upset heifers. Later, after a few bruises and bangs we found the hang of it and finally settled all the cattle in their new homes.

The Italian SS *Humanitos* was formerly the SS *Claus Spreckles* when under U.S. registry during WW II. Length, 427 feet; width, 75 feet; height, 37 feet to top bridge. On this voyage, she had 10,000 tons coal, 160 heads of cattle on main deck area.

CHAPTER 19

An Ocean Voyage

Cowboy's life at sea

In the darkness, with great lights shining down from the masts, we completed our first assignment onboard the *Humanitos*, tired but still excited about our trip to sea. Seven p.m. and we were called to the officer's mess for dinner. (We would discover that in the future, we would eat in the crew mess with quite different fare.)

This night we would have four courses: (1) macaroni soup, (2) fish course, (3) roast beef, (4) coffee and apple pie for dessert. The one disconcerting item was there was no water, only wine. I went without liquid but in the days ahead, I learned to drink wine. There was water onboard but, I guess, the Italians didn't believe in it. The ship's first officer said it was contaminated.

The big surprise was that we had two young ladies as passengers. You can imagine my amazement when I discovered that one of them was the girl who gave me my Italian visa in Washington DC last week. What a coincidence considering the thousands of people in the Washington area!

These two women worked in the Italian Embassy and they were traveling home for a six-month paid leave. We all have a chance to visit the ship's officers, and the ladies. The six of us, cattle tenders, also met each other for the first time this evening. One member of the group, Burk Tassel, was eighteen; so I was not the only boy onboard. The other four were in their 50s and 60s. The evening's discussion was full of scuttlebutt as no one, including the captain, seems to know where our port of entry will be in Italy. (On ending our voyage, we would discover a nefarious reason for this lack of certain arrival port.)

The captain, first officer, radio operator, the two girls, and, of course, the six of us all spoke fluent English; the remaining three officers and the deck crew spoke only Italian.

In the weeks ahead, I would learn enough rudimentary Italian to communicate in a rough way. After this evening, we cattlemen would take our meals in the crew mess. Not one of them spoke English, so it became imperative to plunge into the language game.

A look out the porthole showed a pitch-black night. The ship was moving in the dead-calm waters of the Chesapeake Bay, and all that can be felt was the gentle quiver in the deck plates from the triple-expansion steam engine moving us out toward the open ocean. Later, a look to the north showed the lighthouse on Cape Charles flashing its warning across the dark waters. The ship took on a gentle roll as we passed out to sea, crossing into the Gulf Stream in the darkness. It was time to turn in for the night. I had the top bunk in a compartment located forward, portside, on the main deck. There were three of us cattle tenders in this former WW II gunners' quarters. There was one porthole and a hatch that led to an inside passageway. In a matter of minutes, I climbed into my bunk and was soon fast asleep.

CHAPTER 20

Seasickness

The day was clear with a slight haze overall. Ten a.m. and we stopped long enough to off-load the pilot into the harbor control boat. Wind now began to blow briskly, and the ship took on a roll and pitch. For breakfast, bread and weak wine was all that appealed to me.

Later, after eating, I walked forward to the bow. A beautiful sight greeted me as porpoises bound with effortless ease forward in the bow wave of our ship. On my return to mid-ship, I passed by the windward side. Without warning, a wave hit and sent a flood of water cascading across the deck.

To keep from getting soaked, I grabbed an overhead beam and chinned myself. Not good enough and I got soaked up to my knees. The lesson here was: Don't walk on deck without keeping a weather-eye open for the sea conditions.

The remainder of the day I walked around in shoes that squished. The cattle, housed on the forward deck, were soon soaking wet from the waves that surged across the deck on occasion.

Twelve noon, Thursday, December 4: our location is long 36 deg N, lat. 74 deg W. Mild seasickness was building in my stomach. Some of my friends were not as lucky, as I could see them leaning over the rail trying to chuck up their shoes.

A list of remedies given from other members of our group of cowboys:

- suck lemons
- eat heavily
- take three deep breaths
- walk

- stay out on deck in fresh air
- put head between legs
- **it's all a lot of malarkey that only time will remedy!**

We worked hard building wooden barriers to prevent seawater from entering the cattle stalls. Next, Cattle required feed and fresh stall hay, and so, with all the effort, the seasickness was soon a memory.

Pitchfork man at work

"Mr. Chips" "Carpenter's pay is US $8/month."

It was now evening and after supper I left the crew quarters and reported to the officer's mess. The time had arrived for me to take my last shot for typhus. The captain insisted on giving it. I was sure it was the first time he had ever given an inoculation. It took several tries to get the serum out of the bottle and load the hypodermic needle. Next, the first officer nearly rubbed my arm off with a cotton ball soaked with alcohol. Now, the captain stepped forward like a bullfighter and jabbed the needle straight into the hilt. Holy mackerel!

CHAPTER 21

Hurricane closes in on our course

Thus far, the cattle were holding up well. The only problem was one of the cows developed a case of pink eye. Our group leader was an old farmer and he applied the necessary ointment that soon provided a cure.

The first mate told me we have entered the Gulf Stream because the outside air temperature has had a rapid rise in the last few hours. With this news, we all hoped for good weather tomorrow. As I wrote, the cook came past and watched me chew gum; and after a moment, with the use of sign language, he wanted to know what I was eating. I gave him a stick, and the way he acted, you would think I had given him ten dollars.

In the officer's mess they were eating four course meals while down in our crew mess we are eating what could best be described as slop. Lots of starch and on the side a small piece of meat that was two-thirds gristle.

There was no drinking water, and the first mate told me that water was unsafe. The substitute was a very weak wine. There were five tons on board for crew use. It took me one day before I had begun to drink wine with the rest of the working crew. As the days passed, I was grateful to the person that told me to bring along a small box of citrus fruit. Each day I sucked one of the small stash of lemons that I kept in my locker.

In spite of the food quality, meals provided a jovial time. Conversation consisted of hand signals, pencil drawings, with a sprinkling of Italian that I have learned.

The ship's crew members responded with shouting, table slapping, and a few swear words in broken English. One of the interesting items I observed was that without realizing it people raise their voices when talking to a foreigner. This must be the result of thinking that the other person is not hearing when it is a matter of language not understood.

Once the supper was over, the six of us were allowed to gather in the officer's mess for an evening of discussion with the two women and the off-duty officers.

After several days into the trip, I developed an interesting friendship with Inez Ghiron, the lady who helped me when I visited the Italian Embassy. Her personal history was fascinating. On completion of her undergraduate studies in Turin, Italy, she was sent to complete her education in Paris at the Sorbonne University. (After WW II this university was broken up into thirteen separate schools.) She was fluent in German, Italian, French, and English and had a vast knowledge of Greek and Roman architecture.

With the onset of World War II, she returned to Italy while her wealthy parents moved to live out the war in Switzerland. Later when the Italians surrendered, the Germans held most of Italy captive. As the great battles for the Italian peninsula moved slowly northward, Inez became a secret agent. She passed back and forth through the German lines bringing information to the allied headquarters.

These stories were absolutely spellbinding as she recalled narrow escapes and enchanting escapades with German officers while gathering information.

After two weeks at sea

As the days passed, I learned more about the crew who operated this old rust bucket. The first officer made twenty thousand lire a month. (This equaled fifty dollars per month) The entire crew wore extremely shabby clothes. The teeth of the crew members were universally bad, stained black with lots of dark cavities. I would learn in the days ahead that there was another sinister income that provided their real wages.

Our hope for fair weather was soon just a memory. The sky overhead became a leaden, whirling mass of low cloud. The wind continued to increase as the day progressed.

The waves became higher, and as we crossed over their crests, the ship's propeller came free of the water. The momentary release of the load on the propeller caused cavitations and the entire ship shuddered and shook.

A moment later, we passed into a deep trough and the prop quieted as it dug into the sea. Down in the bottom, all that can be seen was mountains of seawater on all sides. This was followed by a view of the distant horizon as we momentarily hung on the crest of the following wave. On one of these high points, we passed near another ship that was rolling heavily and making no headway. The first mate told us that the ship in sight had lost its propeller and now was at the mercy of the oncoming storm. A tugboat had been dispatched from Baltimore to take her in tow, but it would take two days to reach the stricken ship.

Saturday, December, 6, 1947, Lat 37º N, Long 64.9º W

Our ship was taking a lot of water over the bow and across the decks. Spume flew high over the superstructure as the tops of waves were cut off in the howl of wind. The spent seawater poured down on the ship. The captain ordered the crew to put covers over the air supply vents as seawater was pouring down into our quarters through the ventilation system.

The humidity and temperature inside the ship immediately rose, and the deep roll of the ship made one feel a little queasy. Heavy work constituted the day as we tried to relocate feed in areas free of saltwater contamination.

Later in the night, we returned to our compartment to obtain much-needed sleep. That turned out to be impossible due the strong fear of being dumped from my second-tier bunk. The possiblility of falling several feet down into the several inches of seawater kept me on edge.

The splash of water could be heard as the ebb and flow of dirty water raced back and forth across our small compartment in rhythm with the ship's heavy roll.

Two footlockers that were not tied down continued their crash against the bulkheads. They floated back and forth in the surge of seawater. The ship had taken on a roll that at times completely submerged our one porthole in green water.

Three a.m.! There was a terrible shudder and crash. We were called to go out on deck to rescue cattle. A pyramid wave had crashed down on the ship. (When two waves that run at an angle to one another intercept, they produce a huge pile of seawater that can crash down on top of anything in its path.)

The forward section of the ship was now a mass of tangled wreckage. The wooden stalls were smashed into kindling wood and strewn with twisted tie-down cables. Cows bellowed and struggled to get out from under the debris. The ship's captain turned the vessel to run with the wind and waves.

This action reduced the ship's roll but does nothing to abate the torrents of stinging seawater that flew across the deck. Up on the bridge, the crew turned on the mast lights to illuminate the scene. The six of us struggled to pull planks off the trapped cows and then led them aft to stalls that were not destroyed.

The wind was so powerful that Burk, the other boy in our group, was picked up and thrown far across the deck and landed on his back. Uninjured, he got up to return to the work at hand.

The periodic danger of waist deep seawater surging across the deck required us, at times, to cling for dear life to anything stationary. Pregnant cows floated against us and further acerbated the situation.

We were only able to release a few cattle before the ship's officers, looking down from the bridge, called a halt to this dangerous operation. On the return into the ship, it took two of us to force the door open against the roar of wind.

We gathered in the crew mess hall. One of the two ladies staggered in to tell us that up in the bridge, the wind velocity had just reached 75 mph. (This is the requirement for a full hurricane.)

The other bit of information that probably accounted for her frightened countenance referred to the ship's condition. With each plunge into the running sea, there was a terrific boom like the sound of gigantic bass drum being stuck.

Next, as the bow rose up out of the sea, there followed a second loud pop. She had overheard the first mate tell another officer that one of the plates that made up the ship's bow had broken loose from its internal framework. Now, the only item that prevented a catastrophic failure of the ship's hull was the butt welds that held the plate in position.

I decided to go up to the bridge and see for myself what was in progress. Out in the companionway, I discovered several of the aged crew members down on their knees doing their rosary beads.

Once up on the bridge, the action was controlled and all business. Radio messages were coming and going to and from the captain. The helmsman was in constant motion, holding the ship on its proper heading. The ship was now going in a northeasterly direction. This direction was leading us north of our proposed great circle track. This new track was an attempt to clear the hurricane. Within an hour, the eye of the storm swept over us.

There was a sudden decrease in wind velocity and the rain stopped. Visibility increased and there was a great column of clear air vertically above us. Early morning light illuminated a strange sight. Overhead, a large flock of small birds circled in distress and confusion. Several fluttered down to land in the ship's rigging. One tottered and fell to the deck. This poor fellow was swept into the sea by the next wave over the deck. These birds must have been in migration when they were caught up in the storm. In the calm of the eye, they were trapped and dying. After a short time, we passed through the far side of the eye. The intensification of wind, waves, and heavy rain hit with a vengeance as we continued our heading to the northeast. We continued to pitch and roll, with the constant boom and pop of the loose plate to keep us in the grip of fear. Late in the day, all the storm factors began to decrease, and we broke free of the intense heart of the disturbance.

Once the captain decided it was relatively safe, we were sent back on deck to try and salvage the trapped cattle. After several hours, the six of us plus several of the crew had cleared the debris over the ship's side. Out of this wire and wooden jumble, we were amazed to find only two adult cows with broken legs. They were shot and some of the meat was taken down to the galley. Several little calves were dead beneath the caved-in stalls. There were now forty cows that had to be moved aft. They had to be crowded into existing stalls.

This task took time, as one cow at a time was forced aft through the narrow companionways between the railing and the superstructure. All this was accomplished while the ship ran through thirty-to forty-foot waves. The result was that we were entirely soaked and walked in shoes that squished with every step. By nightfall, all but seventeen cattle had been relocated. Those that remained were tied to the hay bales lashed on top of number 1 hatch cover. I have one narrow escape when on top of number 3 hatch. A wave that I did not see coming swept around me, and I was forced to jump ten feet and grab onto a stanchion to keep from being swept over the side.

Later that evening, Inez invited me to go up to the bridge with her. The officers stood in silence as they watched their instruments record the ship's vital events. Noise consisted of a slight rhythmic creak as the ship's frame twisted as we wallowed forward into the night. The view of the dark ocean was peaceful now. With the storm's passage, we traveled under a black-star filled sky. Out toward the bow of the ship, waves were split, and phosphorescent water curled out to form a lighted path that sparkled on the dark sea.

Sunday, December 7, 1947, Lat 35.2° N, Long 59.9° W

I ate breakfast at 8 a.m., and then went out to feed and water the cattle. Another calf born during the night was trampled to death in the overcrowded stalls. This problem continued daily as the animals had been bred to have their young shortly after our arrival in Europe. Day by day, the cow's birthing agenda fell further and further behind schedule. The cause was late arrival at the Baltimore docks followed by altered course and speed, a result of the hurricane we have just departed.

Later that day, in my off time, I made a wonderful discovery. I climbed high up the forward mast to discover that I can open the hatch into the base of the crow's nest. Once inside, the view provided was of flat azure sea in every direction. With complete solitude, we sailed in the center of a perfect circle. The curvature of the earth provided a uniform distant horizon. Off the ship's stern, our wake appeared as a single spoke, dividing a flat wheel of ocean. We sailed on, suspended between sea and sky. I have always enjoyed having time to contemplate my life. That day the view brought me to the realization that I was nothing but a small speck in the universe. It provided a reminder not to take one's accomplishments too seriously. One hour passed and then it's time to climb back down to clean the animal stalls.

That evening we met in the officer's mess for church services. The Reverend Shear ordered the gathering of our group. He was the minister of our half-dozen cattle tenders. I was surprised to see the two girls, the off-duty ship's officers, and the six of us in attendance for the service.

We all attempted to sing both Italian and American church hymns. In my opinion, it was a rather humorous attempt as the predominant sound is an undulating hum. The gathering was concluded with a short sermon by Shear. The words were somewhat lost on me as I concluded the talk was more posturing than substance on the part of the Reverend.

Monday, December, 8, 1947, Lat 34.4° N, Long 56.0° W

Today was an easy fair-weather passage. We worked hard building new stalls to house the cattle, still out in the open. A lot of sea-soaked straw was thrown over the side in an attempt to provide a dryer environment for our charges. By evening, only nine cows were not covered. Additional cables had been fastened and cinched down over the existing wooden stalls back on the ships stern. Tomorrow, barring bad weather should see the job completed.

Late in the night, I spent time conversing with the first mate. It was a fascinating discussion of cities all over the world that this man has visited. He spun a tale of events punctuated with the men and women he had come in contact with. The faraway ports of call lit my imagination.

Tuesday, December 9, 1947, Lat 34.2° N, Long 51.0° W

We started our routine work early and the schedule of feeding, watering, and cleaning our charges continued throughout the day. The weather became unsettled, and high waves provided our saltwater bath for the day. The cattle were now all housed in rebuilt or new stalls. The last of the hurricane damage was cut away and dumped into the sea. In the past, a sunroom had been added on the rear of the bridge. Yesterday, the last of its shattered remains were removed.

One of the forward lifeboats that had been dangling from a twisted davit was pulled back aboard and lashed down. Once again, the ship looked as shipshape as when we departed Baltimore a week past. The main entertainment was derived from the girls' names being attached to the newborn calves of the previous evening. I was not sure the ladies saw the high humor in this affair.

The feel of tranquility was abruptly broken as the engines' steady beat was stilled. Now we rolled and pitched in the endless wave troughs. A black gang started work to repair some controls on the huge one-cylinder engine. I went below to watch their work in progress. There was a humorous aspect to this event. This Liberty ship had been given to the Italians, and therefore, all the ship's manuals were in English. The mechanics had severe limitations in their ability to read the technical writing. A lot of time was therefore spent in the study of drawings and pictures. After a long bout of gabling and waving hands, the effort commenced.

Two men put tools to work while the other three continued to shout and wave fingers. The result of this event was a delay of eleven hours before we were once again underway on our easterly course.

Another day drew to a close as darkness settled over the Atlantic Ocean.

Wednesday, December 10, 1947, Lat 34.5° N, Long 46.0° W

I awoke to heavy seas and pelting rain. I worked in foul weather until late in the afternoon when we sailed into tranquil waters.

This evening I received my final typhus shot. Thank god, I have convinced the captain not to plunge the needle in like the final stroke of a bullfighter. This provided an end to all my necessary shots for the trip ahead.

The days ahead were routine with only the notations of our position being entered in my day journal.

Thursday, December 11, 1947, Lat 34.5° N, Long 41.0° W
Friday, December 12, 1947, Lat 35.0° N, Long 37.4° W
Saturday, December 13, 1947, Lat 35.4° N, Long 31.0° W
Sunday, December 14, 947, Lat 36.1° N, Long 26.0° W

Sighted three ships today. The first since seeing the propellerless ship the second day out. Two were converging in our direction. The third ship was outbound. The Reverend Shear held church services in the officer's mess once again. Tried to miss the event but I was rounded up by the lead man, Kline. I concluded he thought that I needed more divine guidance. Shear gave half the sermon in Italian, and this provided slight satisfaction to the ship's crew members present. I have a strong suspicion that these people participated due to the captain's orders. They fidgeted throughout the service.

Another night of heavy rain had filled the stalls with two inches of water and muck. We spent the day cleaning and replacing this mush with clean straw. The past several days were recorded only in their sameness. Each day, one or two more calves were born. A few were lost when they were trampled under foot in the deep sludge.

Hard work and long hours makes for good night's sleep.

Scuttlebutt said we would be in Gibraltar in another four days. I can hardly wait.

The six cattle tenders on board the Liberty ship *Humanitos*:

Wilmer M. Kline, Manassas, Virginia
Milford C. Lady, New Windsor, Maryland
Lloyd B. Schear, Lewisberry, Pennsylvania
Burk Tassell, Van Meter, Iowa
Charles Cutting, Campbell, California

For reasons unknown, I did not log in the sixth name.

Sunday, December 14, 1947, Lat 36.1° N, Long 26.0° W

We did the usual cleaning of stalls, hauling heavy hay bales, feeding of animals, and adding fresh water to the drinking troughs. Time to climb up to the crow's nest for thought. It was of interest to me that I was the only one who has made the climb topside. The rest showed no interest in my find. Perhaps it was the long sweeping motion of the mast as we rolled through the rough seas. This place provided me with my own private retreat from the ship's close quarters.

Monday, December 15, 1947, Lat 36.2° N, Long 21.0° W

We had now traveled 2,731 nautical miles since leaving Baltimore, Maryland. Twelve days had past since our departure from the United States. Much banter regarding our proposed arrival in Europe.

Tuesday, December 16, 1947, Lat 36.4° N, Long 15.6° W

I arose to a gorgeous day on the sea. Vibration of the ship's plates and the beat of the ship's steam engine was all that could be heard and felt. I spent a few minutes photographing crew and cattlemen.

We sighted Europe at 4:05 p.m.! We were running south of Cape Sao Vicente, the southwestern tip of Portugal. We are scheduled to arrive in the port of Gibraltar tomorrow morning.

Spent the evening listening to the Sparks's (the ship's radio operator's) tale of being taken prisoner in Puerto Rico *nine* months before the United States declared war on Italy. His ship and a German ship were ordered to turn over their ships to the U.S. Coast Guard. They scuttled their vessels rather than surrender. They were fished out of the water and interned. The tale of being incarcerated in various parts of America riveted my attention.

Later in the evening, I watched the captain jitterbug with our two lady passengers. I was asked to join in, but my country-boy background and clay feet did not cooperate. To save myself from embarrassment, I declined but enjoyed watching some of the others make fools of themselves. I turned in for the night to be ready for an early morning rising.

CHAPTER 22

My first entry into the old world of Europe

In the early morning light, we passed through the Straits of Gibraltar. The famed Pillars of Hercules were in sight. To the north, the Rock of Gibraltar jutted up into the morning sky. Off to the south, peaks of the Jebel Musa stood behind the port city of Ceuta in Africa.

Mythological history stated that Hercules stood with one foot in Europe on Gibraltar and the other foot on Jebel Musa in Africa. In ancient times, great lighthouses stood on the promontories, guiding Phoenician ships on their way. On this day, we glimpsed at Portugal, Spain, and Spanish Morocco, bits of Africa and Europe.

The ship *Humanitos* glided in slow motion into an anchorage in the small bay in the shadow of the Rock of Gibraltar. It was twelve noon, and our anchor splashed down into the oily water. All around us, ships from different parts of the world were loading bunkers for their ongoing trips. Rusty oil tankers with great hoses over their sides fed the thirsty cargo vessels. Just forward of our anchorage laid a sunken British destroyer, a twisted wreck with its bow blown away. The Englishman supervising our bunker loading said that an Italian torpedo plane sank the destroyer in the opening days of WW II. Round about, there were other wrecked hulks of ships shattered by German bombs. High on the face of the Rock can be seen openings from which great guns once protruded. Down at the base, a bustling town is evident. Peaceful tendrils of smoke curl up from stone cottages with colorful flower boxes beneath their windows. It is hard to envision what the chaos of the war years must have imposed on this picturesque village.

I took the ship's launch into town with the first mate and Burk, the other boy cowhand. We went in search of a doctor for Burk. He had broken out with the most hideous boils from the bad starch-and-grease diet of the past month. We found a doctor who gave Burk an injection of vitamins. I was fortunate to have had my box of lemons to supplement my diet. (I had offered them to other cattle tenders, but they had not been interested.)

There was one interesting side effect from my daily sucking of lemons. Over time, the lemon acid had dissolved some of the enamel on the tips of my front teeth. They became sensitive and gave me an occasional shock as when one puts a piece of tinfoil between the teeth. We put back to sea in the late afternoon. To the east in the direction of our course, the sky lowered with dark cloud. The wind increased and started its eerie whine through our rigging. Gradually the sea built up and once again, we were with heavy roll on the rise of swells.

Friday, December 19, 1947, Lat 36° 36' N, Long 2° 10' W

With a few minutes free of duty, I decided to try my hand at fishing. I fashioned a hook out of a bent pipe with an end that I sharpened. The bait was a chunk of cow lung. Next, I played out fifty yards of halter rope and waited. An hour later no success, and it was time to return to work. After I pulled in the rope, there was no bait on the hook, and it made me wonder.

The weather continued to deteriorate. Our workload increased as Burk was still in his bunk with his painful boils, and the five of us now do the work of six.

Saturday, December 20, 1947, Lat 37.9° N, Long 1.7° E

The angry sea built up until we were once again taking waves over the foredeck. The girl, Inez, came out on deck to look around and talk to me. I looked over her shoulder in time to see a rising wave rush over the port side of the ship. I grabbed her and thrust her up against a ladder leading up the side of the bridge. With both my arms locked around her and my hands on each side of the ladder, I held the two of us tight against the bulkhead. The rushing water rose up to our waists with a current that sucked with a heavy pull toward the starboard rail. As soon as the water drained away, she thanked me profusely and rushed back into the ship's interior. I made a mental note to spend more time watching the sea and less time talking to passersby.

I was soon shoveling slop out of the flooded stalls while trying to get newborn calves up on their feet so they will not drown. I tried my hand at milking, something I have not done in ten years. So many calves had been lost that some of the cow's udders were becoming swollen and needed attention. Fortunately, the old farmers took over this chore.

My clothes were soggy, and cold while once again my shoes squished with every step. The heavy shoveling was a blessing as it kept the body warm. Wind gave a shrill whine as it coursed over the deck, bringing sheets of rain from frigid wave tops that have been cut off in the storm.

Then, without warning, a sudden calmness came over the sea. The ship stopped its constant pitch and roll. The wind dropped to a fraction of its former force. The captain has conned the ship in to the lee of the Balearic Islands. The bridge has received a radiogram from another ship a few hours ahead of us in the Gulf of Lions. They were in the teeth of a full gale and have turned to run south in the hope of escape.

Our captain elected to spend the next twelve hours in racetrack pattern in the lee of the Balearics. With the arrival of darkness, we were released to go below and change into dry clothes.

What a relief; it had been a long day and we had skipped lunch. Hot food and weak wine tasted like manna from heaven. The ship moved along on an even keel and there was time for conversation. There was an explanation for the quiet ride on the south side of the Balearic Islands. To our north, there was a great natural funnel formed by the gap between the eastern end of the Pyrenees and the western end of the Swiss Alps. This slot allowed the cold winter storms of northern Europe to race south down into the warm Mediterranean Sea, with hurricane force.

Our captain keeps us in a holding pattern in the lea of the islands shelter throughout the night. On the morning of December 21, we started our run for Sardinia. We passed within sight of Cape Teulads that marks the southern tip of this island.

Monday, December 22, 1947, Lat 39° 40' N, Long 4°, 37' E

We cruised under unsettled weather until evening. Throughout the night, heavy seas kept up a steady pound as the ship's bow crashed through the oncoming waves.

Tuesday, December 23, 1947, Lat 38° 1' N, Long 8° 52' E

Heavy sea state all day made the ride uncomfortable. On occasion, our compartment porthole twenty feet above the ocean disappeared under green water as we heel far over in the turbulent sea. Two calves were born during the night, one drowned in a flooded stall, one cold and wet but alive. Once clear of Sardinia, we steered northeast into the Tyrrhenian Sea bound for Naples, Italy. Now, at long last, our European port of arrival was known. The sea state had subsided and we reduced speed to a gentle crawl. We inquired, but the captain was evasive and would not tell us why. We sensed something unusual was involved.

CHAPTER 23

Strange events of our night arrival

We discovered the reason for the ship's reduction in speed. We have slowed to arrive off Naples at 10:00 p.m. The night sky was overcast, so there was no moonlight and little visibility. The ship's lights, including the navigation lights, were all extinguished. We were requested to return to our quarters and stay until notified by the captain. Burk and I immediately checked that no one was on watch and slipped out on deck and hid in the cattle stall area.

The ship's engine stopped and we glided to a halt. Up above on the flying bridge someone swung a lantern with a white glow. Out of the darkness, we could hear the splash of oars as a rowboat came alongside. In a moment, a few of our crew members arrived on deck, each with a large cardboard box of cigarettes. (We learned the following day that each container cost one hundred dollars in Baltimore and now was sold for the equivalent of one thousand dollars paid in Italian lira. We also learned that this entire operation was under the auspices of Lucky Luciano.)

In the first fifteen minutes, there was twenty thousand dollars worth of contraband off-loaded into the little bumboat. Another rowboat arrived; but no sooner had they arrived, in the far distance we could see some sort of motor launch with a search light sweeping back and forth over the dark water.

Immediately the rowboat cut loose and we started a slow forward motion without running lights. We soon were behind an island out of sight of the distant patrol boat with the searchlight.

This island may be Capri, but I had no certainty. The white light started the process once again. We stopped, and soon, there were three small rowboats ready to receive their order of black market goods. As the boxes went over the side, there was a counterflow of gunnysacks that came aboard from the bumboats. Forward of our position, we could see the porthole that faced outward from the captain's mess. Through the glass, Burk and I could see a flashlight that moved above the officer's dining table. Our curiosity had a grip on us, and we slipped out of our hiding place and proceeded across the foredeck to look into the porthole. Inside, we saw that the gunnysacks contained huge amounts of lira. The sacks were upended on one end of the table while several ship officers counted and stacked the bills in neat rows next to the purser who made notations in a small book that he had opened on the table. We were so mesmerized by these events that we failed to notice two rough figures that slipped behind us. The first realization came when I felt an arm around my throat and the slight coldness of a knifepoint in the small of my back. In moments, we were herded into the captain's quarters. There was a lot of shouting back and forth in Italian. At last, the captain waved the two men off. Since we had seen everything, he told us to watch from the radio room porthole but to stay off the foredeck. Period!

He also said that we were damned lucky that these two goons had not driven their knives deep into our backs. It took several minutes before my heart stopped its wild, erratic beating. The two of us needed no further admonitions to move straight to the radio room. We were surprised to find the two lady passengers already in this location.

None of the other cattle tenders were in sight, and so we decided they had taken the original order to stay in there quarters until further notice. The process of unloading the contraband took several hours. Just before daybreak, a patrol boat came flying around an island and caught our ship in the act of unloading contraband. The neatly dressed men of the harbor patrol raced up the ladder with guns out. There was a great din of shouts from the two groups.

In minutes, the last of the boxes were hustled over the side and down into the patrol boat. The one bumboat that was still tied to our ship was allowed to depart without their boxes of cigarettes. (The next day, we were told that the patrol people removed the remaining boxes of cigarettes but paid only 50 percent of the normal black market price.) I was amazed to learn how business was conducted in this foreign land.

With daylight, the operation was over. The transfer of contraband had started at 10:00 p.m. and it had just concluded 5:00 a.m. I estimated that at least a million dollars had changed hands. More money than I had ever seen or even thought of in my life. This event also answered why so many compartments had been locked with no explanation to our queries. There was a humorous aspect to the story: I had been concerned that my one carton of twenty packs of trading cigarettes would put me in jeopardy. The entire ship's being a black marketeer made a joke of my little stash.

CHAPTER 24

Unloading of the ship's cargo of coal

The ship was tied up at pier 29. This pier is a makeshift affair composed of rubble from the bombed-out dock area. (The docks had been exposed to a thousand-bomber raid during the recent war. The effect had reduced a several-block area to broken concrete and debris.

A lot of this material was picked up and deposited in the harbor to construct pier 29 that we were currently tied up against.) The method of unloading ten thousand tons of coal was slow and unusual. A human chain of men and women walked across wooden planks from shore to ship and then down into the holds. Individuals carried wicker baskets on their heads. Down in the holds, men shoveled coal into these baskets, and the women would move up out of the ship and dump the contents in piles on the dock. These workers were barefooted and wore ragged clothes that were completely covered with coal soot that filtered down from the cracks in their wicker baskets.

To make the task more onerous, they were exposed to a daily misty rain that fell for a few hours each day. This process continued around the clock for five days. (Consider that the ship was loaded with ten thousand tons of coal in Baltimore in a few hours with mechanical conveyor belts.)

My ship unloaded

On Christmas eve, I went into the town to meet Inez, the other woman passenger, and the second mate. It was a clandestine meeting by the Vosovio Stetsion. The ship's captain had tried to organize a drinking party in his stateroom, which none of we four were interested in.

Inez and I went for dinner in a nice restaurant, and the cost was one thousand eight hundred lira with a black market rate of two cigarettes. With the completion of dinner, we spent several hours walking about the city. The other couple went off to find the opera.

During our walk, I was impressed by the view of an old castle that had been built in the twelfth century, long before Columbus sailed for the New World.

Later we had a narrow escape. We walked down a street lined with temporary booths selling fireworks to the throng of Christmas eve revelers.

I noticed a small boy walk behind a stand filled with flares and rockets and set it on fire. In moments, the stand was exploding in all directions, with a roar. Without thought, we were engulfed with the panic-stricken mob on a frantic run for safety. The possibility of falling and being trampled was extreme!

Once I realized the danger, I grabbed Inez by the hand and pulled her out of the fleeing crowd into the archway of a building. After our hearts slowed, we turned and sneaked back to our ship. We arrived back about midnight. All our activity provided enough clandestine adventure for one night.

She was to depart for her home in Turin the next morning, and as she turned into her compartment, she offered an invitation. Would I like to visit her in Turin for a ski trip to her family chalet in Cervinia? (This village is on the Italian side of the Matterhorn.)

I said no but I did take her address with a weak maybe. The next morning after breakfast, she departed, and I felt letdown to see the end of our friendship.

December 26 was a day of hard work. We off loaded all the livestock into trucks that were to transport them throughout Italy. This had an interesting sidelight as it provided me with access to farms all over the country.

The Heifer Project was well known and by way of thanks, I was welcomed to stay in any of the farms that had received one or more of the cattle. The next few days were long, with heavy duty as we cleaned up the decks and demolished the remaining stalls. The decks had to be cleared to allow the hatches to be opened for the removal of the ten thousand tons of coal. The picture shows the ill-clad workmen who worked for several days to hand-carry the coal to dumps across the dock.

Late in the afternoon, I went to town to the police station and had my passport stamped to show that I had entered the country legally. Now I was free to travel through Italy and beyond with the proper documents in hand.

That evening, my fellow cattle tenders left by night train for Rome and Switzerland. We had all been invited to have lunch with Pope Pius XII.

I failed to appreciate the golden opportunity; and as a brash bigoted young Protestant, I said, "Tell him to come down here, and I'll have lunch on the ship with him." How stupid can a young man be?

In the days ahead, I traveled about during the day, and slept and ate onboard my ship *Humanitos* in the nights.

One of my first ventures out was taking an electric train to the base of Mount Vesuvius. I climbed the cinder trail up to the top and then down into the crater.

There was a spooky aspect in the volcano. Every now and then, there was a groan, and the earth trembled a little. Fumaroles emitted the foul smell of gas from the bowels of the earth. I was alone and soon had enough stress from the vibrations and the atmosphere, and I beat a hasty retreat out of the volcano. (A few years after this trip, Vesuvius had an explosive blow up. People are no longer allowed to enter the crater.)

The following day I took the train out to Pompeii. While I waited for the train's arrival, I met another young American. He also worked on a Liberty ship—a sister ship to the one I was serving on. The cargo on his ship was quite different.

Their mission was the retrieval of American soldiers killed during the recent war. I could not imagine doing this task. He said that the cargo holds were refrigerated to keep the odor to a minimum. They stacked hundreds upon hundreds of wooden caskets down in the holds.

We had a great time talking about our experiences at sea and what our plans for the future might be.

On arrival in Pompeii, we surreptitiously joined a tour group and listened to the fascinating history of the excavations. Two things were etched indelibly in my mind: The first was the lead water pipes underground that were still evident thousands of years after their installation. Second, we walked through an excavated home in the red-light district.

There we saw beautiful murals depicting the delights of sexual activity. To a naive seventeen-year-old, this was racy pornography that set the blood to boil. A cold rain arrived and soon put the damper on our ogling. We ran back to the train station to stand under the overhang out of the incessant downpore. On arrival back in Naples, I said good-bye to my new friend, and we each returned to our individual ships.

A short way along the dock, was a small freighter tied to bollards. It was a Russian-registered vessel but had an English crew. (See photo)

I discovered that the ship was destined for Ceylon by way of the Suez. I went on board and located the captain to apply for a job as a wiper or messman. I was hired and told to report at 10:00 a.m. the next morning. That same evening, by good fortune, I met one of the crewmen off the ship in a nearby restaurant. We talked about our lives, and in the conversation, he asked if I knew what the ship did for business. I did not, so he proceeded to tell me that their business was to run contraband guns and ammunition into Yugoslavia. It would be a job of great risk for a young participant.

I was still determined to be on board in the morning. The next item he mentioned was that there was a serious outbreak of cholera in the Suez. Did I think what the consequences could be if I contracted this disease? "They would just have to put me ashore in a hospital," I said.

"No," he said, "you are nobody, a nothing; they would not stop but just throw you over the side during the night!" Thus common sense, and risk evaluation ended my dream of sailing eastward.

In the morning, I did not go aboard the vessel.

Pier 29, Naples, Italy, December 30, 1947

I arose early and started a walk to town to purchase a train ticket to Rome. I heard a strange noise and looked up to see a big helicopter overhead.

I watched in disbelief as the main rotor flew off and twirled this way and that in a slow fall to the ground.

There was a terrifying howl as the engine in the craft wound up and exploded. Parts rained down in my direction, and the main body plummeted to earth nearby with a terrific bang.

Now all was silent. A column of smoke rose from the wreckage in the still morning air. I stood transfixed as I watched a lot of American soldiers and sailors rush to the wreckage.

These military people soon had a cordon around the area, and so I continued my walk into town with a tight knot in my stomach. (Later I discovered the copter had come from the aircraft carrier USS *Midway* that was anchored out in the bay.)

In a tourist office, I was able to purchase a third-class rail and bus ticket—north to Rome, Lugono, Paris, and on to London—for the price of a few liras and a package of cigarettes.

The young man who was my clerk took the money and cigarettes and disappeared into a backroom. I wondered if I had just lost part of my precious contraband, but in a few minutes, he returned with a long voucher that would allow me to get on and off the train at my discretion.

With my future transportation secured, I decided to go window-shopping. In this section of town, there were expensive and elegant shops. There appeared to be little middle ground between this area and the larger, utterly devastated sections of Naples.

Here they were busy in the rebuilding of colorful shop facades and replacing glass in the roof of the great Piazza Umberto. In the same moment, gangs of dirty, ragged people were cooking over small fires amidst the rubble of bombed-out blocks of housing flats.

There was no middle ground; there was either the life of the very affluent minority or the absolute squalor of the poor masses. Because of this stark imbalance, Communism was taking a strong hold on the population.

In the mornings, a lot of hammers and sickle graffiti appeared as paint splashes on the walls of the affluent, as well as the poor, districts. Palmiro Togliatti had recently returned from Moscow and was the leader of this rising movement. In my opinion, it looked as if a bloodbath was in the making. The rich Catholic Church added fuel to the fires of revolution.

Down here in the south of Italy, the church was very strong and drew its wealth from the downtrodden population. They were held in bondage by the fear of God's wrath spread by the Catholic Fathers.

The atheistic communists were quick to point out this fact to the poor and suffering citizens. (In retrospect, I imagine my political view was tainted by a long talk with a Protestant minister who was connected with our cattle-for-relief project.)

In connection with this tragedy of the poor population, I had a narrow escape.

Young boys, I estimated, aged six to sixteen gathered in gangs near the waterfront. Each of these young hooligans carried a stone in his hand. When a lone person came off the dock, these hoodlums tried to get into position to waylay the unwary. (Since my arrival in Naples, I had observed the nude body of a commercial sailor dead in the street, with all his possessions missing and his head bashed in with rocks.)

In my case, as I was walking up a street that led up town, I noticed a group of youngsters started to follow me. I was quick to cut across to the other side of the street and increased my pace. With furtive looks over my shoulder, I realized they had done the same!

With visions of the dead man in my mind, I took to my heels earnestly.

A few rocks sailed my way but fell behind me. With my youth and excellent health, I soon left them far behind.

Now each time I walked from the ship uptown, my head was in a constant swivel. The fear of death makes one weary in the extreme. Fortunately for me, I had not seen another gang on the prowl, but I kept a sharp vigilance whenever I was out for a stroll near the dock area.

My last days in Naples went by quickly. The rest of the cattlemen returned from their Rome and Switzerland junket last evening.

Red, the other young cowboy, and I bought a ticket to Capri for a day of exploration.

It was a lovely isle of the rich and famous. We walked the narrow cobblestone alleys, looking into rock-walled gardens of beautiful summer homes. Our only disappointment was the inability to take a tourist trip in a small rowboat into the Blue Grotto.

The ocean waves that surged against the isle were too great, preventing the small boats from entering the beautiful and famous sea cave. Oh well, someday I shall return and have another opportunity! The sea state was up, and we made for a rough, wet ride back to Naples in the late afternoon.

Our ship, the *Humanitos*, was almost empty, and it was scheduled to sail on Saturday. My free room and board was about to end. The time has come to load my barracks bag and set out on my journey north.

CHAPTER 25

Friday, December 28, 1947, The road to Rome

I woke up to a beautiful, clear, and cold winter day. The second officer of the *Humanitos* accompanied me as my interpreter, and we passed through customs. We then continued to Naples Piazza Municipal; here he left me, with a barracks bag in hand, to board the bus for Rome.

With a twinge of anxiety, I found a window seat and settled down. For the first time, I was a lone American in a foreign land. People around me stared and continued to talk in rapid Italian. I could catch only an occasional word that was comprehensible in my small vocabulary.

The bus wound its way north along the Tyrrhenian Sea coast road. We stopped for a short break in the town of Anzio. I would like to spend more time here as I recalled stories told to me by my uncle Art. He had fought his way ashore here in World War II.

His most vivid recollection was his survival in the rubble of a building that had been struck by a German dive-bomber. In a state of shock, he helped others remove debris from a collapsed hallway. He asked, "Who are you looking for?" His buddies responded, "Sergeant Art Cutting." He said they continued franticly moving broken material for a few more minutes until the realization came that they were looking for him.

The end of his story came when they discovered the remains of a wine cellar and proceeded to get roaring drunk. Today it is hard to imagine the fear and emotions of those days not so long past. I had taken my peaceful life in Campbell as a norm for the world. Day by day, I was getting an education in the results of a far more chaotic life in another part of the world.

The driver of the bus finished his coffee and we all had to load up, and we moved out on the road north. Along the way, we passed over makeshift bridges. A short distance away, we could observe the twisted remains of the original spans. Everywhere, the destruction of war was still evident. The last part of the trip took us near fragments of the Appian Way. It is hard to comprehend that these little stretches of stone-paved roadway were constructed over two thousand years ago. They represent the freeways of the war-minded emperors of Roman antiquity. In California, I grew up in my childhood to think that anything built in the 1850s was indeed ancient.

It was four o'clock as we arrived in the Rome bus terminal—the day's travel completed. Fortunately for me, there were many people who spoke English, and it took little time to locate directions to the American Friends Service Committee center. (They represent the Quaker church that sponsored the cattle project that I worked on.) The office was located in the corner of a large marble building, housing a Catholic nunnery. I was offered a room for my stay in Rome.

January 6, 1948, 44 Via Banili, Rome, Italy

The lodging deserves description. My sleeping room was composed of a space about twelve feet square, all with walls of marble. High up on the wall above the bed was a small crucifix that leaned outward. The only light in the room was a small bulb that was behind the figurine of Christ. This arrangement cast a large dark shadow on the far wall. It provided an almost spooky cast to the room twenty-four hours a day. There was no heat in the building, and I soon noticed the chill that moved up through the marble floor into my very bones.

As an antidote to this condition, I was now clothed in two pairs of sox, boxer shorts, long underwear, pants, tee shirt, wool shirt, sweater, sport coat, scarf, and an overcoat. Rome, in the dead of winter, is not a fun place to live, and it hasn't even snowed yet!

Unless I was in bed or on the walk, my body seemed to be in a continual shiver. This had been a long day, and I decided to forgo dinner and crawl into bed and try to warm up. I tried to write a letter home, but my fingers were so cold and stiff that I gave up on the effort.

I slept well and now got up with the dawn. Down in the basement there was a kitchen with a long table for the people living in the building. There was a big coal stove and oven that had a load of bread in the making.

The warmth (thank god) and the aroma brought my stomach to a hungry pitch. There were eight very attractive young women around the far end of the long table. They were novices studying to become nuns. They were surreptitious in their constant surveillance of my every move. There was a constant titter from their end of the table. After a short interval, we were served a breakfast of oatmeal, bread—just out of the oven, butter, jam, and hot chocolate.

I wondered where they found these supplies, as they were just not available to the general public. Nothing in my life ever tasted more wonderful.

After a very short time, the Mother Superior arrived and sternly ushered the young ladies out of the room. So much for Catholic conviviality! We had not spoken a word of English or Italian, but I supposed that the admiring glances from both ends of the table put the mother off in a most decided way.

I was going on a junket to see the sights of Rome today. The first place to visit was the Coliseum. It was hard to believe the history of this great pile of collapsing stone. According to my tour book, it was built in AD 72 to stage gladiator spectacles.

In its prime, it held fifty-five thousand people. Early this morning, there were no people about the place, so I was free to scramble and explore at my will.

My reverie was broken up when an uninvited fellow showed up and attached himself to me. I tried in vain to tell him I had no money and asked him to leave.

In thirty minutes, I departed—with him still hanging on in the hope of getting money. When he finally realized there was no reward in the offing, he gave me a very dirty look and muttered a few unintelligible (Italian) words, and departed. I was sure the words were nasty, but his leaving made me chuckle. Every place in Italy seemed to be packed with beggars that follow foreigners in hope of getting cigarettes or money.

My next stop is St. Peter's Square and Basilica. I have a chance to enter the catacombs. Inside the entrance to St. Peter's Church was a great hole in the floor that workmen had recently opened.

I met one member of an American University archeology team who were working in conjunction with an Italian group. After a short discussion, I was invited to pass under the roped-off area and descend down a rickety ladder into a section of recently opened catacombs.

Crude wires trailed down through the opening above to provide electricity for naked lightbulbs. It was very cold, and there was a lot of dust in the air. Several men were in the act of using small brushes to remove dirt from artifacts they are uncovering in the wall niches. My newfound friend explained a little of the history of the items now, after centuries, being exposed. One man has just discovered a small pottery object, and the preliminary consensus was that it once held oil and a wick to provide light. My guide was called further down into the tunnel. I don't want to be a hindrance, and therefore, thanked him and took my departure.

Once on top, I went to search for the Sistine Chapel. I was alone as I walked through and studied the beautiful artwork that adorned the walls and ceiling of the magnificent hall.

(Forty years later, I returned to see the Sistine Chapel. It was so packed with people that it seemed you could raise your feet and be swept along with the mob. At age seventeen, I had a unique European experience in a time after the second World War, before the hoards of world tourists arrived.)

Piazza Venezia was my next stop. Prior to the war, my uncle Ralph (he had fought the Germans in the battle of the Argonne Forrest) would say, "That bastard Benito with his buddy Adolf will get a lot of us killed." I was more interested in building model airplanes, and his agitation did not really register in my young mind. Later, I clearly remembered newsreels clips that preceded the cowboy movies at Saturday matinees. These Pathé news clips in the early part of WW II would show Benito Mussolini standing on the balcony of his headquarters on the Piazza Venezia. Seeing the strutting dictator of Italy shouting to the masses of his people was indelible in my mind. Today all was silent; only a few passersby were in the street in front of that infamous location. I stood quietly in the street below and thought of the war years that America had seen.

Later back at the Friends Service Center I had a very interesting conversation with Devere Allen, who was a columnist for an American newspaper. He seemed knowledgeable about the present political events taking place in Italy. We spent an hour after dinner, and he filled me with the political news of the present.

January 8, 1948, Ortona, Italy

Today I had the opportunity to ride with some of the Americans that lived and worked in the Friends Service Center, where I was presently staying. They were driving in an open jeep across the Apennines. This is the mountain chain that runs the length of Italy. Our destination was Ortona, a village on the shore of the Adriatic Sea. The day was clear and cold as we climbed up the highway to the east. One spectacular scene followed another as the snow covered mountains appeared as cutouts against the sun, rising out of the east. I viewed several tiny villages built on top of the surrounding peaks. They appeared dark and ominous as they were outlined by the snow-covered hills. I was told that these hamlets were originally built in the Middle Ages. They were constructed on the peaks as protections against marauders. To this day, there are stacks of boulders around their encircling walls to provide protection. If there was fear of a threat in the night, the boulders were let loose to crush invaders. A few German troops were harmed in this manner during WW II.

The road we traveled was in reasonable condition, but a jeep is a rough-riding vehicle and that, coupled with the freezing air, made for uncomfortable travel. After we crossed the high ridge of the mountain chain, we drove down toward the sea. The air became warmer as we descended from the mountains.

At the base of the mountains, the town of Ortona lies in the narrow margin formed between sea and foothills. During the fight to occupy the hamlet, it was hammered by artillery from the hills and battered by heavy naval guns from the sea. Now the rubble of Ortona was in a gradual rebuilding process.

During the battle for Italy, the Germans initially occupied the town. It was the anchor to the Gustave Line that the retreating Germans built to stop the Allies on their push for Rome. The port of Ortona was the Axis's supply port to reinforce the Gustave Line. After intense bombardment followed by hand-to-hand street fighting, the New Zealanders drove the enemy out. In turn, the Germans retook the town only to be driven out by the English, and once again, the town changed hands.

The waves of battle flowed back and forth several times before the Allies took permanent possession of the town. This was an important seaport that was needed to resupply the troops that occupied the region. The result was a bloody battle that lasted weeks and devastated the town.

In the afternoon, we arrived at the quarters that would be our home for the next two days. The building that we stayed in was over two hundred years old and had been used as a field hospital during the war.

Our room was on the second floor. It was an interesting location in that the entire side of the building, including the staircase, had been blown away. To reach our room, it was necessary to climb a makeshift ladder constructed of a tree limb with rickety crosspieces nailed on. Our sleeping quarters were, indeed, unique. The entire east wall was missing. Once at ease in our military cots, we had a clear view of the city spread out below us. In the near distance, the blue waters of the Adriatic Sea washed back and forth through the bomb-shattered breakwater.

Another item that caught my attention was the absolute stillness of the city. Outside our missing wall, there was an old olive tree with a lone grave beneath. It had a wooden cross with a German helmet hung on top. This poignant scene drove home to me the brutality of warfare. No matter the right or wrong of a battle, it brings to mind the terrible finality of a family's dear lost son.

Today we went to various locations to view the renovation work of the Friends World Service projects. There were many Americans here who devoted their lives and talents to aid the needy in this war-shattered country. They certainly have my admiration. I worked a few hours with others to remove debris from a town well. Later we had a supper of stale canned bacon and eggs, all washed down with gritty powdered milk. In the evening, we all discussed our thoughts on the fragility of life. These ideas I had never considered in my sheltered life at home in Campbell, California. I realized that this whole trip was one continuous educational experience.

The men from the Friends Center completed their inspection trip to Ortona. The following day, we loaded our personal effects back into our rugged little jeep and started our return trip to Rome.

Our quarters in the seaside town of Ortona, Italy

On the return trip, I was dropped off in an Italian Boys Town in Lanchano. A gentleman named Don Guedo ran this little way station in the mountains. This man had a fascinating history. During WW II, he escaped from German-held France (this occurred after the Italians changed sides).

He made his way through enemy lines, and after several months on the run, he arrived in North Africa. With the termination of the war, he returned to Italy and founded this small Boys Town. The inhabitants were all orphans, many of whom carried the scars of war.

The place was truly amazing as the boys all worked to rehabilitate each other under the care of Guedo and an associate. All the youngsters were learning a trade. Shoemakers, blacksmiths, cooks, woodworkers, and other trade workers all lived and worked together with great camaraderie.

The older boys supervised the younger. There were few cardinal rules. Stealing was not allowed, but on the other hand, they could have fistfights to settle grievances. They all lived and survived with minimum essentials of daily life. They made do with broken tools, little food, and rooms that are open to the elements. I was impressed with the selflessness of these two men who gave their lives to the betterment of these boys.

On preparing to leave, one of the young boys gave me a small sample of inlaid wood that he had fabricated. (I still have this piece of wood in my footlocker fifty-seven years later) It is beautiful workmanship for a young teenage youth.

This morning I took passage on a rickety old bus back to Rome. One amusing event took place on this trip. We stopped in a town for a thirty-minute break. I needed to use a restroom but did not know the word in Italian. I rushed around in a frantic state but could not locate the required facility. In desperation, I stopped a man on the street, and as a last resort, I patted the front of my pants in hopes he would understand my dilemma. He smiled a very helpful smile and led me to an official-looking building. We climbed two flights of stairs and entered a room with several men waiting in line for a doctor. I suddenly realized that I was standing in a prophylactic station. In a state of acute pain and embarrassment, I rushed out and down the stairs to the street. I had the best and longest pee of my life at the first dark alley that I came to walk in.

The rest of the day was a long, tired ride back to Rome. Once back in the service center, I located a friend who provided me with the word for toilet, *gabineto*. I don't think I shall ever forget this magic word!

CHAPTER 26

Saturday, January 10, 1948,
Rome to Turin in freezing winter

I boarded the Rapito Train for Carrara, and using my trusty single cigarette bribe, I was moved up to a first-class seat. With the pass that I had purchased a few days earlier (also with the aid of cigarettes and a small quantity of lira), I was in great luck. The ticket I held has many segments that went all the way to Victoria Station in London. The pass confused the conductor and he said in broken English that he had never seen one like it. He further stated that as far as he can tell, I could get off and on at my discretion along the route.

The train followed the coast of the Ligurian Sea. I dozed and woke to see the picturesque villages along the edge of the water. There was a temporary stop in the town of Pisa. I discovered that there would be a later train on to Carrara, and on the spur of the moment, I left the train to walk to the Leaning Tower of Pisa.

Pisa is an ancient university town. One of its most famous inhabitants was the astronomer Galileo. In this present age, the Leaning Tower Pisa brings the most notoriety. The tower's construction first began in 1173 and continued for many years. (This period is hard to contemplate for a Californian. We consider our Spanish missions as old, and they date to 1776 in San Francisco.)

The tower is actually a cathedral bell tower. Its recent history is tied with the WW II battle for Italy. The town of Pisa was the anchor point for the Gothic Line built by the Germans. The Axis (that's what we called our enemies) used the tower as an observation post during the forty-day siege in 1944. A lot of shell damage could be seen on the structure. I paid a small fee to enter and climb the 293 steps to the top of the tower. I feel a little spooked as the top is tilted seventeen feet from the perpendicular. I said to myself, *This place has been here for centuries; certainly, it won't fall down now.* But I didn't feel confident until I was once more on the ground looking up.

The train for Carrara did not leave until 7:00 p.m. With an hour and a half of free time, I located a restaurant for dinner. I consumed a good meal of spaghetti and salad. Once again, I was onboard the train for the two-hour run to Carrara. In the gathering darkness, we traveled north into the Apuan Alps.

It was 9:00 p.m. as I clambered off the train in Carrara. The weather was cold and damp that January night in northern Italy. I was coming down with a severe head cold so I was anxious to locate the Brethren training center. This organization was part of the relief effort that I worked for on the cattle ship. They were very hospitable, and I was soon sound asleep in my own room. The next morning after breakfast, I saw the results of their work. Three hundred kids arrived to learn the art of sewing and woodworking. They took a break from their studies for an hour of sport activity. After physical education, they filed in for a free lunch provided by this relief organization.

In the afternoon while the children were back in school, the distribution of clothing to needy people of the town proceeded without pause. (When I was driver's helper back in New Windsor, this was one of the destinations of the bundles of clothes that we delivered to the New York docks.)

American volunteers—all married couples—sign for a two-year term to man the local center. They were provided with board and small homes at the cost of seven dollars per month.

I spent the next few days in my room, trying to shake off my head cold. On the third day, I felt well enough to venture out to visit some of the world-famous marble mills on the hills nearby. The marble of Carrara is said to be of the highest quality in the world. From the time of Michelangelo to our present era, the world comes here to buy their marble supplies.

In the display rooms, there were examples of statues, tombstones, and wall sections of pure white stone. This industry is by far the most prosperous that I have seen in my travels in Italy. The demand in the postwar world seems unquenchable. The sad fact is that the rest of the nearby country was terribly impoverished.

On January 15, 1948, My cold is much improved and it's time to move on. At 6:30 a.m., I boarded the train from Carrara to Turin. The train was filled predominantly with second-class passengers.

In the moments just before departure, there was a mad rush as all the second-class passengers pushed up into the first-class coaches. The conductor blew his whistle and yelled, but no one moved; so in disgust, he walked on through the train.

I had thought all along that I wouldn't stop to see Inez, my lady friend from the *Humanitos* Liberty ship, but now, with two weeks on my own, the idea of seeing her became a lot more appealing. Therefore, the plan today was to go to Turin and look up Inez.

The train sped north along the Gulf of Genoa. The tracks hugged the coastline and the views were spectacular. The bright sun splashed into the sea, turning it into a collage of vivid blues and greens. Out on the sea, slack brown sails of fishing vessels bobbed in the swells.

This spectacle was momentarily broken as the train plunged into long dark passages through the cliffs above the sea. While in a tunnel, vision was blotted out and sound became the dominant sense. The train engine produced a roar that was punctuated with the rattle of iron wheels on steel rails.

Add to this the constant jerk and sway of the car and one soon looks for the return of horizon and daylight. Along the right-of-way were bits of war debris. Smashed equipment and bridges showed the effects of heavy aerial bombing.

Four hours passed and we entered the seaport of Genoa for a short stop. Time to buy some bread from a vendor on the platform. My meal was torn pieces of rough-grain bread, spread with the contents of a small can of tuna that I brought from Nevada in the months past. Passengers poured off and on the train. The locomotive emitted eddies of steam in the chill air as the train idled on the spur beside the main line.

After a few shrill whistles from our engine, the train started its slow chuff forward. Soon we were accelerating northward up the main line toward Turin. The train gained elevation, and now patches of snow started to appear along the right-of-way. Clouds began to form overhead, and the cold became intense. The coach provided little heat, so I pulled out a sweater and another pair of pants in an attempt to combat the chill that invaded my body. Other passengers throughout the car also pulled on more clothing to ward off the cold.

We arrived late in Torino in a foggy cold afternoon. In the terminal, I located a phone and called Inez and was told she was out. I needed to get out of the frigid weather and soon located a small hotel. For one U.S. dollar and a cigarette, I had a room in the Albergo Genoa Torino. The only drawback was the pungent smell of the freshly painted room in the damp, cold air. To escape the odor, I went out to walk about the town. The industrial part of town was devastated from the frequent heavy bombing during the war. Walking through the residential section of town, I discovered there were occasional small areas that were all smashed to bits. I suspected that this was the result of a bomber missing its target in the industrialized section of town.

A five-hundred-pound bomb load from a B-24 or B-17 can certainly level a block of apartments.

On returning to the hotel, I made contact with Inez and was invited to come to her home for dinner. For a country boy from Campbell, California, the home was an eye-boggling experience. The three-story mansion covered a third of the block. Stone, marble, and tile covered the outside of the building. A butler came out to the ornate iron gate and directed me into a huge sitting room where I met the family. The father was a portly gentleman while the white-haired wife was just a slip of lady. They spoke a little broken English while Inez and a younger sister spoke fluent English.

I was made welcome while a flurry of maids came and went in the final preparation of dinner. The meal was of many courses that even included roast turkey. It was a real effort not to gorge myself after so many months of small portions of poor food. On completion of dinner, we removed to the library for coffee and cake. With the two girls interpreting, we had a general discussion of current world events. While we talked, it came out that Mr. and Mrs. Ghiron had moved to Switzerland and spent the war in this neutral country. He was an industrialist and somehow he was allowed to do this with permission from Mussolini?

This entire evening was fascinating. While I looked on, another peculiar event occurred. Mr. Ghiron requested one of the waiters to bring his cigarettes. In a few moments, he was handed a small box that was filled with half-smoked American Camels. I was informed that these were an item hard to obtain. While I watched, he reached into the box and brought out a matchstick with a needle stuck in the end. He proceeded to place one of the cigarettes on the needle. After he lit the butt, he proceeded to smoke it down to a point where a further inhalation would have burned his lips. I was awed with the value placed on American cigarettes in this country. No wonder Lucky Luciano was heavily involved in the smuggling of contraband smokes.

For the next few days, I was in and out of the Ghiron home. On one occasion, the father wanted to show off some of his hidden wealth. He removed a painting off the wall that covered a hidden safe. Out of this strong box, he showed me a roll of one-hundred-dollar bills. He wrote on a piece of paper "$16,000.00." This was followed by a small bag of diamonds worth fifteen thousand dollars. I was certainly impressed but felt this act was very childish on his part.

This brought to mind my own financial condition. I had at that time about fifty U.S. dollars and ten thousand lira (worth about seventeen dollars), plus a few packs of cigarettes. In the afternoon, I sent a telegram to my parents to wire another one hundred dollars from my stash. By my account, they should have a little over three hundred dollars left in my account. To save money, I made the telegram short and sent it.

Inez had made arrangements for a skiing trip to the Alps. She gave me the details, but I balked when I discovered that it will just be the two of us. "Oh, I don't think I should do that." (How naive can a young man be?) She says, "Okay, I have a friend, Luciana, who will go with us." This afternoon the three of us bought bus tickets from Turin to Cervinia. This ski resort was located in the Alps on the Italian side of the famous Matterhorn.

CHAPTER 27

Tuesday, January 21, 1948,
I learned to ski and other things

Inez, Luciana, and I arrived in Cervinia at a small chalet owned by the Ghiron family. Unfortunately, it had been unoccupied for some time and was freezing cold. The three of us spent a miserable night, and in the morning moved down the hill to L'Albergo Astoria hotel.

Money was becoming a problem so I requested to stay up in the attic where the help lived. The management gave me the okay; so for the next few days, I would sleep up above. The hotel was beautiful with big windows that looked from the dining area across to snow-covered peaks. We were assigned our own table with a gorgeous view. There was a big recreation room with a record player with lots of American swing records, a small dance floor, billiards table, and shelves full of books. (A few of them were in English.)

The first snag arose when I went out to rent ski equipment. Skis were no problem but when I tried to find ski boots to fit, I was out of luck. Apparently, the Italian men have small feet and I needed Italian size 45.

Inez talked to the instructor, and they locate a pair at a nearby hotel. In a few minutes, they were delivered, and I was out on a beginner's slope. A helpful soul came up to give me instructions, and amidst the sitzmarks through trial and error, I began to make progress. I stopped for lunch, and the two girls joined me in the hotel restaurant.

We had a conversation about the condition of the trail from the top of the mountain where they off-loaded from the gondola lift. My goal was to come down that mountain after another day of practice. The afternoon was spent learning to snowplow and the art of gentle turns. By evening, my Levi's were soaking wet, but I was getting the hang of staying upright most of the time.

Just before returning to the hotel, the Alpenglow played across the north side of the great triangular Matterhorn peak. I thought of my artist grandfather who would have soon put this ethereal view to canvas.

By the time supper was served, I was cold and exhausted. It was amazing how fast one can recover with a hot shower and delicious, hot mountain food. We spent the evening dancing and talking with the few people who spoke English. Later, I climbed the servants' stairs up to my bed under the eaves. A flood of morning sun through the lone loft window acted as my alarm clock. There was only cold water in the morning, and shaving was no fun, but it *was* bracing.

The ladies were already having breakfast at our table when I arrived in a semistarved condition. I tried not to appear ravenous, but after the hard workout and the mountain air of the day before, all the eggs, ham, toast, jam, and croissants were soon gone. After a few minutes of talk, we were on our way back to the slopes. I saw them off on the gondola and returned to my learner's hill.

After a few minutes, an older ski tutor, who was between students, came over to visit. Last night, I had talked to him about his experiences in World War II. He had been captured in North Africa and spent two years in Arizona as a prisoner of war. Because of this experience, he was fluent in English, and we had enjoyed a long talk last night. Now he offered to help me in the art of skiing. After giving me some instruction, he returned to his students, and I practiced what he taught me.

When he completed work with those students, he came back and picked up where he had left off. The day passed in a rush. I had far less falls than the previous day and felt that I now had the basics in hand.

I arrived for dinner at our table to discover that Luciana was missing. I asked what happened. Inez just said that Luciana had fallen and twisted her ankle. She had taken the afternoon bus back down the mountain to the train station and was on her way back to Turin. I was sorry to hear of her troubles but was so hooked on skiing that I wished that we could stay longer as originally planned.

Inez said she had hoped that I would want to stay. That night we danced, and my friend, the ski instructor, insisted that we drink wine with him and his girlfriend. It was my first encounter with wine drinking. (On board the *Humanitos,* we had water that was cut with a small amount of wine to prevent stomach sickness from the bad water.)

This was an entirely new experience! The evening was great fun as we danced and reveled in front of the great fireplace. Later in the evening, Inez said, "Take me to my room."

She opened her door, and I leaned over to kiss her good night, but she took my hand and drew me into her room.

Later, I left to return to my attic room. In retrospect, it would seem funny to me. I was sure that the other fellows that lived in the attic would know what I had been up to, and with that in mind, I crept with slow, careful steps up the staircase. I spent fifteen minutes in the short climb up to my room, not daring to make a sound. On reaching the landing in the dark, all that was audible was the heavy snoring of the other men. It came to me that they were not in the least bit interested in my business.

In the morning, I came down to breakfast ready for a new experience. We talked about the evening, and she spent time to explain some of the things women liked and didn't like. I was so unsophisticated that I needed all the help that was available. One item that bothered me was that there was a couple that sat near enough to hear our conversation. Inez could see my unease and said, "Don't be silly. They don't speak English so we are perfectly safe to talk on any subject." I decided she was right and gave it no more consideration. We had a long breakfast and talked of many subjects from sex to Italian history. The view was idyllic with the sun cascading over the snow-covered peaks.

I was ready to try my luck on the high trails. With only a day and a half of instruction, it would be a quick transition from the little hill behind the hotel. We boarded the gondola and rode up to a station several kilometers above the valley. We exited the cab, and I took several deep breaths and then pushed off downhill. Fortunately, there was a gentle way down for those who were still in the learning stages. Some of our lift companions shot over small cliffs of snow and moguls with whoops and hollers and were soon tiny specks on the trails far below.

With our older fellow travelers, we traversed back and forth down the well-groomed trail. What an incredible feeling to glide down the mountain with only a peek at the skies through the light film of powder snow. I was pleased to only fall once when my skis became crossed.

On occasion, I flailed my arms wildly to keep from a fool's flop in the snow but somehow kept on the move. The farther I traveled, the more control I gained and the faster I went. It also became easier to make turns while keeping more weight on the uphill ski—an advice that Inez shouted as we laughed and frolicked down the hill.

On arrival back at the hotel area, the ski instructor came over to congratulate me on my success. He told me that he didn't think that I would be able to make the trip with so little instruction. The day went by all too fast as we made several more trips down the mountain. Fatigue became more of a factor as the day wore on, and I took several more spills. Fortunately, I hurt nothing more than my ego.

This evening we sat and relaxed over dinner, and Inez and I talked over a wide range of subjects while our neighbors at the near table chatter away in Italian. After a time, we returned to the subject of bedroom possibilities and I became more at ease as the couple at the next table appeared to take no notice of our conversation.

After dessert, we met the ski-instructor couple and spent a convivial evening of talk and dance. Once again, Inez was a great instructor as I was sort of a bumbling country boy with little experience on the dance floor. Now and again, we traded partners, and the whole evening was one of great camaraderie. I thought I shall never forget this night in the high Italian Alps. Later, Inez and I retired to her room. What a romantic view with the moonlight sparkling over the snow-covered mountains!

I must be learning something because she was as happily engaged in this tryst as I was. It's now 3:00 a.m., and after one last kiss, I left and made my slow, silent climb up the stairs to my bed under the rafters. Once again, I was greeted with the sound of loud snores. I was sure they could care less what I have been up to; but with my naivety, I crept around like an idiot before silently climbing into my cot. Once again, it's the sun, through the small window high up on the clapboard wall, that awoke me for breakfast. All my roommates were long gone to work by the time I rose to wash and shave.

I met my friend for breakfast, and we were soon out on the slopes enjoying another day in the cold mountain air. This will be our last day as we were informed this morning that a huge winter storm was expected to arrive tomorrow night. We cannot afford to become snowed in for a week, so it will all end too soon. Between the skiing and the lady, I would like to stay forever. The day and night passed in a wink of time.

The following morning, we were down early for breakfast. During the night, five inches of snow had fallen. The road out of town had a fresh coat of white. Our bags were packed and propped by the heavy oaken door, ready to be picked up by our bus driver. Heavy snowflakes were cascading down outside the dining room windows while we ate our last breakfast in this winter wonderland. There was a pause in our conversation when the gentleman with his girlfriend, sitting at the next table, got up and came over to my side and spoke in perfect English. "Young man, I think that you will never forget all you learned on a wonderful vacation on the back side of the Matterhorn mountain; be good and enjoy the rest of your life."

With that, the girl who was with him went into unsuppressed giggles while I turned beet red in my acute embarrassment. The couple arose and walked out of the dining room. Even Inez chuckled and said, "You are such a lovable country boy."

In a few minutes, we were onboard the bus as it slipped and slid its way down the mountain. The driver told Inez that in another hour, we would have been marooned in Cervinia. Now we were on our way back to Turin. I could not believe it was over. I was sure I shall never forget these few golden days!

CHAPTER 28

January 27, 1948, Money problems arise

The previous fall on leaving California, I had taken a hundred while leaving three hundred dollars savings in my bank account. My idea was to send for some of this cash as needed on the trip. I had earned additional dollars with the work for the Heifer Project Committee in New Windsor, Maryland. This I had done while waiting for my cattle boat to Italy. I now ran out of cash and was in desperate need of a money resupply. Prior to our leaving for skiing in the Alps, I sent a telegram to my mother asking for an additional one hundred dollars from my account. There was no reply, and so I had sent another message to the same effect. Imagine my surprise on my return from the mountains when I realized there was still no money. I took lodging in a small pension near the railway station in Turin, but I had not enough money for another day of rent or food. I talked to Inez explaining my predicament, and she came up with a quick fix. She called an old family friend in Paris and requested that he call her father at home requesting that he come to Paris on some bogus business problem. Mr. Ghiron departed that night and I moved into a spare bedroom in their home that evening. I already had my train ticket to London but without any money, the food would be a real problem. I immediately wired my grandparents as follows.

WESTERN UNION
CD TORINO VIA WUCABLES 25 26
NLT FRANK CUTTING=
93 HARRISON AVE CAMPBELL
SANTA CLARA COUNTY

**MOTHER DIDN'T ANSWER TWO TELEGRAMS
PLEASE TELEGRAPH ONE HUNDRED DOLLARS
IMMEDIATELY CHARLES CUTTING
MERITBANK TURIN ITALY THANKS WELL=
CHUCK
JAN 27 1948**

To my immense relief, the money arrived the next morning. Once again, I realized how fortunate I was to have grandparents who were always ready to give me support when needed. They could contact my mother for reimbursement. Now, again solvent, I departed aboard the next morning train for Lugano, Switzerland.

CHAPTER 29

January 31, 1948, Winter Olympics, St. Moritz

Anxious to get underway, I boarded the night train to Milan. I arrived late in the day and spent the night in room near the railway station. I had time to stroll through the business district before collapsing into bed. This northern part of Italy was amazing after the time I have spent in the south.

There seemed to be no war damage in the downtown area. The shops are full of expensive items and crowded with well-dressed citizens. North Italy had always been the industrial base of the country. Lots of wealth centered here as opposed to the poor agrarian hard-scrabble south.

It was a pleasure to walk the streets at night without the constant necessity of looking behind to stay clear of muggers that seemed to abound in the southern towns. I returned to my room to rest before my morning trip to Switzerland.

A short train trip from Milan took me through the beautiful Alps and deposited me on the edge of Lake Lugano. I rented a room near the town square for five Swiss francs. Cigarettes were not valuable as they were in Italy, so I have to use some of my cash. The city was very friendly and many of the citizens spoke English, so I was soon out sightseeing along the edge of the lake.

In the afternoon, I boarded a lake steamer and traveled down to a small village for lunch. After eating, I located a trail behind the restaurant and spent the next hour climbing up to a location that provided a spectacular view down the distance of the lake. The blue of the water was broken only by the wakes of an occasional small steamer that connected the small villages with transportation.

The stillness of the afternoon was broken now and then by the loud caws of two crows that seemed to be following me. On reaching a viewpoint, I realized my time was up and I needed to return to catch the afternoon boat back to Lugano. I passed the only other person on my trip up and down the mountain.

He was an older man, with gray hair, a weathered face, and carried a gnarled walking stick and is followed by two dogs. His clothes were of well-worn rough spun fabric. He carried a leather rucksack that appeared to be full. Where was he going? Up to a mountain hut, or just out for an afternoon's stroll?

We passed by each other and smiled but he did not break his pace. He must be in wonderful condition as he traveled uphill almost at the speed that I was walking down. The dogs didn't bark and stayed close to his heels. By the next bend in the trail, he was out of sight, and I was left with no answers.

It was interesting to me that there was no snow in this lake valley. The picturesque tile-roofed houses were often surrounded by gardens that contain plants that were almost tropical. How can this climate exist in the Alps?

Someday I would like to return and spend a month or two in this mountain hideaway. Now it was necessary to run the last hundred yards to catch the steamer that was about to depart. On the trip back to my hotel, I had an interesting conversation with a U.S. military man and his girlfriend who were down from Nuremberg, Germany on leave. They were involved in the trials of Nazi war criminals and had many fascinating stories to tell. They invited me to have dinner with them, but I knew on my meager budget I would be embarrassed so I decline.

That evening near my hotel, I was able to buy a round-trip bus ticket to St. Moritz. The fifth Olympic Winter Games was in progress and I passed up dinner to save money for the trip. I bought an apple and croissants with a bit of cheese, and I had an adequate supper.

I left a 4:30 a.m. wake-up call for the next morning to catch my bus transportation to the Olympics. The route took us to the east back into Italy for a short while and then up into the Swiss Alps once again. I had purchased food, similar to last night's dinner, for my breakfast and lunch for today.

The bus arrived about nine, and I walked a short distance to see Canada and Great Britain play hockey. Lots of rough and tumble play, and in the end the Canadians won 3 to 0. This was the first time I have ever seen hockey. I was amazed how they could twist and turn and stay upright even as they crash into one another.

I met a U.S. Army major while watching the match, and he offered me a pass to box seats to watch the ski jumping event later in the afternoon. It was a wonderful opportunity, and I was happy for the chance.

As the hockey ended, it started to snow. I only had a light sweater over my shirt and was I ever cold! Fortunately, there was a hot-coffee-and-snack bar with an overhang where I was able to take shelter. In front of this shop was a giant sculptured snowman put up by the Coca Cola Company. It was huge and very unique. Lots of tourist took turns standing in front of this snow statue while their friends snapped pictures. (I suspect the photos didn't turn out well because of the falling snow.)

Within half an hour, the snowstorm blew past and we were once again in the sunshine. I whiled away the time waiting for the ski jump event. Walking around the Olympic Village, observing the elite international tourist crowd, was fascinating. I had never seen or heard of such ostentatious people in my little village of Campbell, California.

Later I met my major friend, and we boarded a military bus that took us to the ski jump venue. The first class box seats gave us an unobstructed view of the athletes as they soared off the jump to land far down the slope. I had seen newsreels of ski jumping, and they always seemed to crash and cartwheel.

That was typical news propaganda of the movies. In reality, we watched for an hour and only one contestant fell and did not cartwheel. An American won the day with a jump of 68 ½ meters. (The world's jump record was by a Finn: 81 meters in 1928).

Later I watched the end of the downhill racing and found it much more interesting than the jump contest. That the contestants could stop in a short distance after passing the finish line at high speed was a sight to behold.

In the late afternoon, I boarded the bus for my return to Lugano. The bus was warm and a blessing to my frozen feet. I was shod in oxfords—not the required footwear to tramp about in the cold snow. My head was soon on my chest and the trip back to the lake was lost in sleep. Back in my hotel room, I packed my bag for the onward trip tomorrow.

CHAPTER 30

Monday, February 2, 1948,
On to Basle and Paris

I departed Lugano on the 9:30 a.m. express train for Basle. This leg of my adventure was, without doubt, the most spectacular in its beauty. Outside we would fly along a beautiful, limpid lake lined with small villages with a town steeple presiding over the tile-roofed cottages. With a sudden rush, we would be in a dark tunnel with only the shrill train whistle to break into one's thoughts.

Next, we would burst out into the brilliant sunshine. Outside, the train passed through a narrow glacial canyon with steep sides that reached up to the snow-covered peaks above. Again, we plunged into a dark tunnel through the rock spurs that seemed to support the high cliffs. Out once more in the clear and we are in a wide valley.

The roll of the hills was covered with deep green grass. Bands of sheep, watched over by a lone herder and his two dogs, were out in the meadows. An occasional low gray-stone hut with smoke rising from the chimney spoke of a quiet pastoral life in progress.

I had to spend two hours in Zurich before the next train would depart for Basle. I walked through the business-and-shopping district to pass time. In all of Switzerland, the stores were full of wonderful and expensive goods. This country's neutrality in WW II gave them the opportunity to make great profits from the conflict. They sold goods and services to both sides.

On this subject, I was told one interesting story about this practice. The Swiss were selling a lot of essential war material to the Germans, and the Americans, of course, took offence to this business.

A letter of complaint was sent through the embassy and after a few weeks without any change or response, an American air armada flew in and leveled one of the Swiss industries that supplied the German war machine. The Americans sent an official apology stating that the American bombers had accidently flown off course; the Swiss got the message loud and clear, and they stopped supplying the Germans.

I boarded the noon train for Basle. En route I met a fellow passenger, a young lady returning from a visit to her grandparents in Zurich. Bridgett was Swiss but she could speak perfect English, and so we struck up a conversation. I made a date to meet her later in the evening in Basle. This evening, we went to see an American movie, *Saratoga Trunk*, and finished with a coffee in one of the little cafes on a side street.

She worked in a leather tannery where they made expensive women's purses. One sad sidelight to this occupation was that her hands have turned walnut brown from the constant emersion in a tannic acid solution used in the curing of the leather.

I was quite taken with her persona. She speaks fluent French, German, and Italian. This was quite common with educated people in Europe but unheard of in my California home. We talked about our families and our hopes for the future. One of her hopes was to visit the United States, and she and I exchange addresses. We talked on until late at night and then she said good night with a promise to meet for dinner the following evening. I put her on a streetcar and she disappeared in the dim glow of city streetlights. It would be a long wait for tomorrow night.

I stayed in the Hotel Vogt and Flugelrad at room 22 where breakfast is included in the sixteen eighty Swiss francs per night. I rolled this way and that in my bed while thinking of this wonderful girl. All kinds of possibilities weaved through my smitten mind.

I got up early for my breakfast and read a single copy of the U.S. military *Stars and Stripes* newspaper that I found on a side table.

One article that attracted my attention was in regard to the Russians. With the end of WW II, they made a land grab of East Germany. One item that angered America was the control of Berlin, the former capital of the German state. On the conclusion of hostilities in 1945, Berlin was divided into four parts. The Americans, French, British, and Russians each had partial control of the city.

This city is located 200 miles into East Germany, and the Russians were threatening to storm the city and throw out the Allies. Europe was in great tension over this impending crisis. There must be some GIs staying in this hotel as most of the papers were in German, with this one exception. I looked around the small tables but didn't see anyone that looked to be a fellow countryman. With my croissants, cheese, and tea finished, it is time to get out to see the local sights.

Today has dawned bright and clear, and I walked through the town, window-shopping and people-watching. The local housewives were out on their morning chores. The food supply stores were quite different than our typical California grocery store.

There were small shops for each food item. A greengrocer sold fresh vegetables, while a few doors down the street, the fabulous smell of fresh baked bread filled the morning air. Still further on, fresh-butchered geese and hams hung in the window. Wine shops and milk stores were each in their own little storefront. The meat was a pleasure to see, as it was not covered with flies, as was the usual case in southern Italy.

There were no paper bags, but instead, each lady carried a cloth or leather carrier that she loaded with local produce. Once loaded they all seemed to have a couple of long baguettes sticking out the top as they returned to their apartments. Meanwhile, I looked in on a few ancient churches, but to me, they all seemed the same, with their statues and loads of bric-a-brac hanging from the walls and ceilings.

I soon tired of damp, dark church museums and moved once again out into the warm sunlight. My walk took me down a narrow cobblestone passageway that opened out on the bank of the Rhine River.

I located a dock and walked out to the end where I could sit with my feet dangling above the water. There was a constant parade of working ships and barges, on the move up and down the waterway. It was possible to navigate this river all the way north through Germany and Holland and end up on the English Channel at Rotterdam.

Today, barges filled with gravel, coal, and produce passed in review. Some of the tugs that pulled these barges had families living on them. Small children waved at me as they passed by. In the stern of one boat, a lady was doing her wash. I thought this would be an interesting lifestyle, always moving through water while viewing the change of season and scene outside your door.

After lunch, I had the distinct impression that I was being followed! I zigzagged through several streets and occasionally stopped suddenly and turned to look behind me. Yes, here was a tall man in a felt hat following me. What could he possibly be doing this for? I decided to return to my hotel room and decided on what to do next. On entering my room, it was evident that someone has gone through my personal things. Now this made me angry, and I looked out my window to see the tall man standing across the street ostensibly reading a newspaper.

I left my room and went down to the lobby and found a rear exit out of the hotel. I skirted around the block and came up behind the watcher. Quietly, I reached out and tapped the man on the shoulder.

He gave a great jump and turned to look at me. His face registered shock, and I asked him in English, "What the hell are you doing?" He didn't say anything; he just folded his paper, turned, and walked off hurriedly.

I returned to the hotel and wrote on a piece of paper, which I folded and placed in an envelope. Inside was a description of the fellow who was following me around. I was concerned that if something happened to me, there would be no record of what I knew. I requested the hotel desk to keep this note in a safe place until someone asked what has happened to Mr. Charles Cutting. The note read:

> Caucasian man
> Light complexion
> Deep wrinkles on forehead
> Height about 6'2"
> Eyes a bright blue
> Dark blue suit
> Gray felt hat

A date with my beautiful Swiss girl was only a few minutes away. I cleaned up by putting on my remaining clean shirt and combed my hair. I once again left the hotel by the rear exit and started for the place to meet Bridgett.

Each block that I passed, I stopped and looked back to see if I was being followed. No, there was no one to be seen in my wake. I guess the city police or whoever had lost interest, as there seemed to be no further surveillance of my movements.

I arrived at our agreed meeting place on time, and to my great pleasure, she was there waiting for me. The night before, she had told me of quaint little restaurant on the bank above the Rhine. Off we went, and after a few minutes, we were there.

We sat out on the veranda and listened to the rustle of the river as it swirled past our vantage point. She was like a dream to me with her blond hair and clear blue eyes. Her complexion was like fresh peach, and when a sudden wind blew her hair back and a few drops of rain sprinkled her face—well, anyway . . Out across the water, the lights of passing ships twinkled and made the waves dance and sparkle. Our talk traveled over all manner of thoughts and dreams as we held hands. A more idyllic setting would be hard to find.

Inside the inn, we had a splendid dinner of roast beef and many side dishes. Time seemed to take wings and we floated in a bubble of tender rapport.

The unfortunate fact was that I was due to take the train on to Paris in the morning. We walked back to the trolley line in silence, our arms about each other. We stood in the darkness near the streetcar stop in close embrace. We whispered softly to each other that we shall meet again in America. Then the streetcar clangs to a noisy halt in front of us, and with a final kiss, she climbed onboard and was swept away into the night.

I walked back to my hotel, terribly sad and depressed. I tried to think of solutions but there were none that made any possible sense. Sometimes being a young man can be terribly painful! I know, I know, my mother would laugh and say, "You suffer from a severe case of youthful infatuation." Maybe so, maybe not—anyway it's finished.

Six-thirty and I boarded the high-speed train for Paris. We rushed kilometer after kilometer at breakneck speed. After a few miles, I lost sight of the Rhine River on our right. The scenery was not very interesting as it was flat and with little vegetation. Open fields that were all plowed up for spring planting. There were not even the flocks of sheep that I had seen throughout my Swiss travels—just empty space.

Once in France, I could see traces of the recent war; great bomb craters appeared near main rail junctions.

CHAPTER 31

February 4, 1948, Paris, France

On the train trip down from Basle, I met an American GI on vacation out of Berlin. We had a great time shooting the bull about our lives. You can imagine my surprise when I discovered that he was from San Jose, California.

On arrival in Paris, I departed the train, looking for a place to stay. My new acquaintance said he was going to the Ambassador Hotel and so I followed along. I decided to stay even though the price for a single room was expensive. This place was like nothing I had seen before. Electric eye doors swung open as you approach. Rich upholstery on the furniture spoke of money. I requested a cheap room, and the desk clerk was nice enough to rent me a very small room up in the attic. The first hour I spent walking around the premises. Great public rooms were adorned with Old World paintings that covered the walls. I came across a reading room with racks of the world's newspapers available for the patrons. I found a copy of the *Paris Tribune* in English, and I sat down to catch up on world news. America was in smooth postwar transition. Articles indicated my nation was peaceful, and business was expanding. However, Europe was another matter.

The Russians are saber rattling over Berlin. People were actually selling their property and moving west, away from the Russian zone of influence. War was in the air, and many people were frightened! I wondered if I should get out of the Europe as soon as possible? No, I was not going to panic like a chicken.

The next day I strolled and rode trolleys through Paris. I started my walk by passing through the Arc De Triomphe. This huge 150-foot high arch was erected by order of Napoleon. It was dedicated in 1836, and the sides depict the great military victories of France. Under the arch lies the body of the unknown soldier of World War 1.

To the French, it was a most sacred monument. I could remember in 1940 watching RKO movie clips of the victorious German troops goose-stepping through the arch while the local populace stood in silence with tears streaming down their faces. Today it has regained its former glory.

I took a short walk down the Avenue Des Champs-Elysees, and I stopped for coffee and croissant in one of the many street-side cafes to people-watch. Well-dressed women and men in all types of apparel passed by. The men's clothing ranged from shabby workman's blue denims to suits of the finest material. Everyone seemed to have a mission as they moved in rapid pace past my observation post. It seemed strange that I saw not a single child. Tables around me seemed to be occupied by the older, less-hurried set. Grizzled and knurled groups of old men sat and talked in animated tones. Sometimes they even shouted at one another. How I wished I were able to understand their conversations. There were few apparent tourists other than American GIs. It was midwinter, and tourism had not picked up since the war's end. Finishing my hot coffee, I felt warmed, and I started down the street with my guidebook in hand.

Next place of interest was the Obelisk of Louqsor (called Cleopatra's Needle), located in the middle of the Avenue Concorde. It was a gift to the country from the Viceroy of India in 1836. From reading the hieroglyphics on its sides, scientists claimed it to be thirty-four centuries old.

I took time to run my hand over the rose granite said to be constructed in the ancient time of Rameses the Great. It was more than I can comprehend. In California, we think of the Spanish Missions that are fewer than two hundred years as being very antiquated.

The most interesting facet of this area was that at the time of the French Revolution there was an equestrian statue of Louis XV on this location. This statue was destroyed and a guillotine was erected. Louis XVI, Marie-Antoinette, the Duke of Orleans, and two thousand citizens were executed during the Reign of Terror. I recalled in my reading of the *Tale of Two Cities* in Ms. Gardener's high school senior English class. This is the joy of education—when one can travel and put location into the context of the written word.

The sun in the east told me that I walked in an easterly direction down the Rue de Rivoli until I reached the Louvre. Once the home of monarchy, it is now the national museum of art. How I wished my artist grandfather could be with me now.

Inside, I viewed *Whistlers Mother, Mona Lisa, The Bohemian*, a self-portrait of Rembrandt, and many other famous paintings. I felt overloaded with information and decided to get out into the fresh air and move on.

My walk took me along the bank of the Seine River. For a time, I was content to sit on the embankment and rest my tired feet. While I took a respite, a constant parade of river traffic passed by. This waterway is a main artery of transportation for the city of Paris. Resuming my walk, the church of Notre Dame came into view. I crossed a bridge that took me to the island on which it stands. Fortunately, I met a man who was fluent in English, and he pointed out that they were installing stained-glass windows in one corner of the church.

During the war, all the glass was removed and stored in a safe place in the event Paris should come under bombardment. Now two years after the war has ended, they were still in the process of reinstallation. I took a quick look inside, but I was not interested in the religious artifacts and soon moved on. I took a streetcar that took me to the Montmartre district. I walked up and down the narrow streets and looked in the shops and starving artists' galleries. This area was fascinating with an assortment of ladies of the night, winos, and outrageously dressed drifters. I stopped long enough for a cup of coffee in another street-side cafe.

After a few minutes of watching the local people, I continued up the hill to the Sacre-Coeur de Montemarte; from the veranda of this ancient church, I looked out over a spectacular view of the city of Paris, framed by the setting sun. The lights started to wink on in the city as I made my way back to my hotel.

I had made arrangements to meet my American GI friend to attend the Folies Bergere later this evening. I left a wake-up call for 7:30 p.m. and flopped down on my bed for a much-needed nap. When the telephone rang, I got up and splashed cold water on my face and went down to the lobby to meet my friend and several other GIs that had gathered for a trip to the theater.

The show was a new experience for a boy from the country. Beautiful ladies in scant costumes swayed in swings overhead while chorus lines of gorgeous synchronized girls gave-eye catching high kicks. This activity brought on cheers, whistles, and yells from the GIs. A famous black lady, whom I had never heard of, sang songs in French. She was an American entertainer who came over to Paris just before the war. She stayed on and worked for the French underground. Now she was idolized in France. The whole evening's entertainment was exotic and certainly a new experience for me. Later the GIs left to drink up the town, but I demurred; I had no money or interest for such activity. I thanked my San Jose friend and returned to my hotel room for a much-needed night of rest.

Friday, February 6, 1948, Eiffel Tower, Paris

The day was raw and uncomfortable. There was a high solid overcast, and a strong wind howled through town. I dressed with the addition of a sweater and a heavy black overcoat. After lunch, I arrived at the Eiffel Tower. The elevator took a crowd of us up to the second landing. (In the 1940s, this was as high as one could go by elevator.) This was not what I had in mind when I first viewed the tower yesterday. It was my intention to go to the top at 910 feet (276 meters) above ground.

The tower was built in 1889 for an exposition to glorify the French Revolution. This event ushered in the freedom of France from Royal oppression one hundred years earlier. Mr. Eiffel was the engineer that designed the Suez Canal, and this was to be his final effort. At the time of construction, the tower was the highest structure in the world. It is a latticework of steel beams completely open to the wind and weather. In 1918, the government added a radio tower on top with a little enclosed room for the technician to monitor the radio transmitters.

Today I studied the steel fence that blocked further movement to the circular open staircase that leads upward. I was thinking about how to pass this obstacle when a young Canadian GI came up alongside. We struck a conversation, and I mentioned to him that my intention was to climb to the top. "Let's do it." His name was Ted Kapitula, and he was a Canadian navy boy from Ottawa, Canada. We started to figure out a way to bypass the barrier. We went to the end of the fence and climbed up on the safety railing on the edge of our viewing platform. Using the last fence post as support, we were able to lean out over space and round the barrier. The wind was now blowing so hard that our overcoats stood out behind us like Batman's cape. We started up the spiral staircase as the whole tower shook and shuddered in the gale-force wind. After a climb of about one hundred feet, we looked down to see a uniformed guard yelling something to us in French. We pretended that we didn't see him and continued to climb upward. With the howl of the wind and the constant shaking of steelwork, we gripped the stair rails so hard that our hands turned white. Up, up we climbed ever higher. There were 1,650 steps to the top, and we were breathless as we neared the little enclosed room at the top.

A man came out of the door and started shouting and motioning us to turn around and go down. We were within fifty feet of the top. He was red in the face from shouting and gesturing as he followed us down the long staircase. There was a small gate that was unlocked, so we didn't have to hang out in space to pass the steel fence. We met three men in uniform, and they escorted us down the elevator to a small room for interrogation.

There was one English-speaking fellow who wanted to know what the hell we thought were doing, and so forth. The interrogator did explain that the little man in the radio room could not get the door open in the force of wind until there was short break in velocity. That was the reason we were able to get up so high before he was able to intercept us.

After twenty minutes of haranguing, we were told to get out and not come back. Once out of sight of these men, we had a good laugh over our high adventure. We stopped by a small bistro for a coffee and croissant. After an interesting conversion about our time in Europe, we each went our separate ways.

There was one last interesting event that took place while I was in France. There was a devaluation of the French franc. In the morning when I awoke, it took twice as many francs to pay for anything that you purchased. I did not care as I was to leave for London later in the day, so I only lost a small amount of money when I exchanged my last French francs for British pounds. The loss was even less when I realized that a lot of my buying had been done with my small stash of cigarettes. Here, as in Italy, tobacco was a great currency.

CHAPTER 32

Saturday, February 7, 1948,
On to London, England

I left Paris at twelve o'clock noon and rode the train north toward the Belgium boarder. Before crossing out of France, the train veered west to the port city of Calais. Railroad cars were rolled onto the train ferry, and at 4:50, we set sail across the Strait of Dover. The high winds that had buffeted me on my climb up the Eiffel Tower were part of the storm that continued to howl southeast out of the North Sea. High waves rolled out of a black sea and sky as we pitched and rolled toward England.

After fifteen minutes, many passengers were lining the rails feeding the fish. Fortunately, I still had my sea legs, so I stood out on the deck and let the sea spray fly over me. Arriving in Dover, a locomotive was attached to our railcars, and after a few short blasts on the train whistle, we were on our way to London.

I had called my aunt from Paris, so it was a welcome sight to see her standing at trackside when I arrived at Victoria Station. In a few minutes, we were onboard the four o'clock commuter train for her home in Sutton, Surry. She did not realize that I had just missed her on her *Queen Mary* departure from New York back in November.

She laughed at my scrambling down from the Empire State Building only to see her ship pull out into the channel. We talked of our travel of the past few months and soon were in the High Street Station in her hometown of Sutton.

It was wonderful to see my four girl cousins whom I had never met before. They had prepared a hot meal of roast beef and potatoes for dinner. Later I would discover what a treat this dinner was in a land where wartime rationing was still in effect. I ate like it was my last supper while we talked and became acquainted.

My Aunt Helen Sturges' home in Sutton, Surry, England

My relatives owned this spacious old home during WW II. (My uncle Tommy was away in Africa during the war years, engineering a railroad to bring out a mineral that the Allies could use to produce aluminum. I remember well his occasional arrival in our California home on one of his worldwide junkets. He was filled with tales of working in dense jungles and barren deserts. He would keep me spellbound with tales of natives that might do great harm to the intruding white men.)

In the rear garden was an earth-covered bomb shelter. The family had spent time in there during the great Battle of Britton air campaign. From their back garden, they had watched the contrails that swirled off the dueling German and English aircraft.

Another interesting item was the bombed-out building just down the street. It had been hit by a doodlebug—German V1 flying bomb that the Nazis shot into England toward the end of WW II.

This home belonged to an old retired admiralty lawyer, and he was killed at the time. My aunt and some neighbors went out that night to collect memorabilia that were blown out into the wind and rain. She picked up a sheepskin velum that had been written in the time of King James and signed by his exchequer.

To hold this document in my hands brought a real sense of history. It had been written in the 1600s!

I settled in for a three-week stay with my relatives. My cousins took me to London on day junkets to see the city. There was great evidence of the recent war. Lots of condemned buildings propped up with huge timbers to keep them from tumbling into the streets. Occasionally, there were streets blocked off to foot traffic.

City workmen have uncovered another unexploded bomb and the disposal squad will be called out to dispose of it. Once we heard a great boom and were told that a bomb had been detonated as the only way to get rid of it safely.

Another sight that was gut-wrenching was the passage of small groups of physically impaired war veterans. Caring military nurses led these men about the town. I could see that many of these people were horribly disfigured.

Without the aid of these caregivers, they could not bring themselves to go out in public alone. The object of these walks was to hopefully build self-confidence into their shattered lives. I think the price of war was hard for someone of my age to comprehend. We must leave our safe little towns and villages to actually see the wanton destruction of men and towns—the horrific price of war!

Airfields

I rode the train from my aunt's home in Sutton out to the old international airport of Croydon. I could remember well the newsreels of Neville Chamberlain (English prime minister) getting off an airplane at Croydon as he told the waiting newsmen, "We shall have peace in our time."

He had returned from a meeting with Adolf Hitler after the latter had just reoccupied the Rhineland. Today, the field had only a few small aircraft, and industrial buildings were crowding in all around. London Heathrow had taken over as the international airport and Croydon was weathering into oblivion. I was free to walk around to look at the few old derelict aircraft that were no longer airworthy.

A few days later, I traveled out to Redhill Airdrome. What a fascinating place to investigate! It had been an RAF fighter base that was lent to the free Polish Airforce.

Around the perimeter of the field were a few wrecked Spitfires. Two of them still had bullet holes through the fuselage that must have happened during the recent war. Another one had one wing and landing gear bent beyond repair. While I was studying this aircraft, a fellow walked up to talk to me. He had been a mechanic on the airfield and told me that the Poles were careless pilots. They wrecked a lot of aircraft in landing accidents, and this was what had happened to this plane.

On the other hand, he said they seemed to be completely fearless fighter pilots, and therefore, shot down more than their share of enemy aircraft. This was one of my favorite pastimes, talking to men who were participants in the battles of WW II.

Now the field was a glider training port. The British government subsidized pilot training for young people, and someone told me about this program. Today I had come out to investigate. For the princely sum of ten pounds, a boy could stay for two weeks while learning to fly a primary glider.

I rushed to fill out the papers and provided the necessary ten pounds to participate. We were to stay in old RAF quarters, and meals were also provided.

The class that I would participate in would not start until Easter vacation. However, we were free to walk about and watch those currently in training. On this day, there was a low overcast with a hard wind blowing, so there is no flying.

Another fellow and I were told that we could sit in a glider seat and try to keep the wings level if we liked. The machine was held fast into the wind with a short rope to an iron picket pin. With the strong wind that was blowing, it was possible to keep the wings level by the use of the control stick.

After a little trial and error, I was able to lift the wings up to a level attitude while the skid was, of course, still in contact with the ground. The problem was the intense cold. After a few minutes, my hands turned white in the freezing wind and my feet went numb. I had to give up and run into the hangar to stand next to the coal-fired, pot-belled stove to thaw out.

As soon as I came in, the other fellow would run out and take his turn. We kept this up for about an hour and finally gave it up. The hangar had instructors and students standing in little groups talking about the dos and don'ts of the actual flying. I stood enthralled, trying to soak up all the information that was being bandied about. Late in the afternoon, I departed to return to my aunt's home in Sutton.

This was the type of glider used in the training program in progress. Several boys pull the aircraft up the hill by hand. At this point, a wire is attached that runs downhill to an auto winch in the valley at the foot of the hill. When all is clear, the winch engine starts up and the operator clutches in and the wire starts to pull the flying machine downhill. The student in training keeps the wings level as he scoots down the hill. With the continuation of several lessons, he is pulled faster and faster until he, at last, gets airborne a few feet off the ground.

At this point, he disconnects the cable and glides on down to the flat land below. Because the glider is a single seater, it is necessary for the instructor to stand on the hillside and yell instructions through a megaphone. This was a primitive, but effective, method of flight instruction.

I was in a constant state of euphoria waiting for the call from the airfield that my class was ready to start.

It was not to be!

Two days before the class was to convene, a telephone call came in to report the sad news that both gliders had crashed. My dreams were crushed, and I moped about for a few days. I consoled myself with the promise that I will certainly fly one day. (As it turned out, within a few years, I would not only become a glider instructor, but also, with the aid of a friend build a sailplane from scratch in his backyard. This machine would be far advanced from the fragile glider that I sat in the freezing wind trying to keep the wings level in 1947 in England.)

In addition to the loss of the gliders, a strong storm had blown in from the North Sea, bringing a foot of snow in the last four days. My cousins talked me into going to the International Ballet in town to escape the ever-present cold. The cost was four shillings and six pence for Orchestra stall JJ27. I can't say I think much of the semiclad young people who jump and spin about on stage. I suspect: once a farm boy, always a farm boy.

I decide to return to mainland Europe, and in preparation, I made several trips into the heart of London to obtain visas for Belgium, Holland, Denmark, and, for the future, a final one for Brazil. My aunt Leona had relatives in Jutland, Denmark and she had previously written that I might arrive on their doorstep.

CHAPTER 33

March 5, 1948, Leaving Sutton Surry, England, for Belgium

I departed Sutton at 6:30 a.m. for Victoria Station in downtown London. My ticket was third class in a coach next behind the engine.

The price was right, but the accommodations were spartan. Outside, a thick coal-induced London fog obscured everything. In addition, smoke from the locomotive swirled in a tight cloud of choking vapor that infiltrated the coach.

There was a great deal of hacking and blowing of noses from the foul air in our compartment. We sat on hard wooden seats, and after a dark weary time, we arrived in the port city of Dover.

Eleven a.m. and it's time to board the channel steamer *Albert Kroner* for the crossing of the Strait of Dover to Ostend, Belgium. The ride was quiet, and the sea was smooth as glass. I spent the four-hour crossing up on the first-class sundeck.

There was no sun showing through the heavy overcast. Occasional patches of heavy fog provided an echo chamber for the continual plaintive blasts of the ship's foghorn. I spent the trip in conversation with a Belgian man who was married to an English lady. I am forever amazed at the conversational topics of total strangers.

For the best part of an hour, he explained in detail the sexual habits of his wife and English girls in general. On arrival in Ostend, his wife was waiting for him, and without an introduction, they rushed off arm in arm. With a teenager's mind I can only imagine the results of their reuniting.

I boarded a bus for Brussels and looked out at a land that was absolutely flat. At the moment, there was a constant hard wind. It must be the usual weather for the few trees evident were all permanently bent in a downwind direction.

I had been told that there was a YMCA in town, and I made my way there. With my trusty barracks bag in hand, I arrived at the front desk. First, I inquired if there was any room available for this weary traveler. Yes, they had an annex that was a military barracks during the war and was now used as a hostel.

After cleaning up and a taking good night's rest, I asked if they could recommend some of the places to see. They not only had a list of things to visit, but there was also a young lady who would act as guide for no charge for the opportunity to practice her English.

That is how I came to meet Mary Louise Huygens. I offered to take her to an outdoor lunch in the square of the Guild Halls. We had a great lunch while telling each other a little of our life history. She explained the background of the Hanseatic League that operated in these buildings.

This organization was founded several hundred years ago to protect and promote trade in the region. (Today we have Lufthansa Airlines—that means "air traders.") After a walk around the town square, we took the *G* tram out to Gaesbeek Castle. This is a beautifully restored fortress and moat that once formed part of the town's defenses.

We walked into the museum to look over the collection of early weapons used to defend the area from marauders. Going up onto the parapets and into the towers made the time fly.

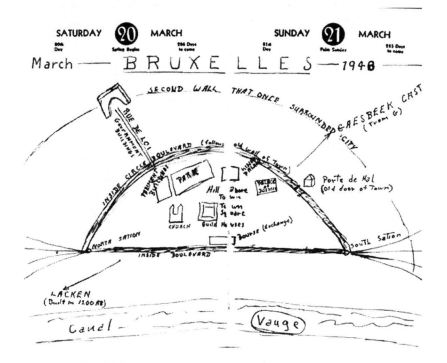

My hand-drawn plot of the old city of Brussels.

When we return to the YMCA, she invited me out to her home for evening dinner with her family.

I met her father and mother and brothers, and they were all interesting people. One brother spoke English, but the rest of our conversations required Mary Louise to interpret for us.

It was still early as we made our way back to my barracks quarters. She made an interesting and surprising proposal to me as we rattled along in the streetcar. Because it was extremely difficult for a Belgian to get to America, she had this idea. Would I marry her?

She said I did not have to sleep with her or anything else unless I wanted to. As my wife, she could enter the United States and become a citizen. Once she became a U.S. citizen, we could get a divorce and go our own ways.

It was a shock to receive such a proposal, but I was not about to come home a married man and, therefore, declined the offer. She was not in the least put off, laughed, and said it was worth a try, as I seemed a nice man.

I did offer to send her *Jazz at the Philharmonic,* a record she would like to add to her collection. We parted as good friends, and with that, I returned to my room in the barracks.

This is a picture of my guide, Mary-Louise Huygens—and would have been my wife, if I was so inclined!

The dormitory that I stayed in was a youth hostel ran by the Brussels YMCA. There was a real mixture of young men. The room I was billeted in has three other nationalities. A Dutch, Polish, and Belgian made up my roommates. They all spoke English to a degree.

The Polish fellow was in his early twenties and was a remarkable man. He spoke Russian, Polish, Dutch, French, and English fluently. He was very unassuming but was willing to talk about his life. He was in the Polish cavalry (horses, that is) when the war started in 1939. His squadron was sent out to oppose the onslaught of German tanks and infantry. In the second week of fighting, he was shot out of the saddle and ended up as a prisoner of the Bosch until 1945.

His stories of trying to escape through tunnels built under the prison compounds kept the other three of us on the edges of our bunks. He was fortunate to have survived, as those who were caught tunneling were often executed in front of their fellow inmates.

Another time they had almost completed a tunnel when the Germans discovered the plot and purposely blew up the escape route, burying his friends alive. With his release on conclusion of WW II, he went to work for the U.S. Army. They were in the business of gathering information for the upcoming Nuremburg war crimes trial.

Here in Brussels, he was applying for immigration papers through the U.S. embassy. I told him I hope he makes it, and I gave him my home address in Campbell. What a surprise it would be to see him in the future!

The Dutch boy had been captured in Surabaja, Java, in the early days of the war. He was pitifully thin, and I suspected his health was poor. He returned by ship a few weeks past. He spoke English but was very quiet and reserved. He had talked a little about the terrible conditions of his incarceration by the Japanese but, in general, was very silent. He had said nothing about what his future plans might be.

The young Belgian was spending time here in the capital trying to locate remnants of his family. This was all that he would disclose. He did not want to talk about where he came from. The three of us were interested but respected his privacy and did not pry further.

This morning, I took the W tram from Place Rouppe out to the battlefield of Waterloo. I knew very little about Napoleon Bonaparte's famous battle with the English hero Wellington in 1815. I was extremely fortunate to take up a conversation with a distinguished-looking gentleman. He was an elderly American history professor from Harvard University. I suspected he sized me up as a needy history student. The next four hours we spent walking over the surrounding countryside while he lectured on all the phases of the famous battle. In his briefcase, he carried maps that we laid out on the ground while we sighted the various locations of the struggle. We climbed to the top of a man-made hill in the center of the battle area.

On the 180-foot summit there was a great lion made from the melted-down iron of French guns. The hill was constructed eleven years after the battle.

The engagement lasted two days and saw fifty-three thousand men killed and wounded. Legend claims that the widows of the Englishmen built the hill by hand. A lovely story, but I somehow doubt its authenticity.

Late this afternoon, the professor and I stopped in a small inn for lunch. He wanted to hear my story, so we spent time on the details of how I had arrived in this place. We moved into a discussion of the current European political situation.

He added excitement to my interest in the war clouds that seemed once more to be rapidly gathering over Western Europe. We said our good-byes and exchanged addresses with the hope of one day meeting again. He was a fine fatherly figure, and I had thoroughly enjoyed the day.

This evening I was invited out to dinner with a friend of my Campbell high school football coach, Mr. Drummond.

During WW II, Drummond worked for the Office of Secret Service (OSS) and had parachuted into occupied Belgium to work with the underground. He had been hidden in the home of these people for several months while he reported to London on a clandestine radio. (They were setting up operations to go into effect on D-day.)

The people whom he stayed with were very hospitable to me and wanted to hear all the news about their wartime hero.

We had an interesting visit about their exploits in and around this area. My host raced motorcycles as a hobby, and that created an opportunity to discuss one of my interests—auto racing.

Dinner was steak—one of the few since leaving home months ago. What a wonderful evening!

CHAPTER 34

March 11, 1948, On to Holland

Yesterday I returned my unused Belgian francs and bought Dutch guilders for my onward trip north. Once on board the train, we traversed mile after mile of flat farmland. Not much of interest in this winter month.

The only evidence of the war was the bomb craters that were often seen alongside the railroad tracks. All other devastation had been repaired, leaving no scars of the war. Out the train windows, we saw only the start of spring grass and a few scraggly sheep in the pastures.

It was a cold and dismal day when we arrived in Amsterdam. My first need was to locate the YMCA for lodging. The place was a regular hotel with a few rooms in the back for the Y. I rented the room for four days for ten guilders. This fee also included breakfast at no extra charge.

Prior to letting me sign in, the lady in charge gave me a stern lecture on the necessity of no roughhousing and quietude. She explained that the hostel was paid for in effect by the fees charged to the regular hotel guests, and they must always be considered.

I was assigned to a large room with three other boys. Once again, this turned out to be a most interesting group of young men. They all spoke English to some degree, so we soon made our acquaintances and related our separate stories. Later, we all trooped down to a separate mess hall and had our fill of bare essentials: boiled potatoes, spaghetti, thin meat sauce, and over-cooked cabbage.

Early the next morning, I was off on a walking tour of the town of Amsterdam. I bundled up with long johns and heavy scarf to keep the penetrating cold at bay. The city was built on marshy land. Poles driven into the soggy ground supported the buildings.

There were a series of ten canals circling the city. Each one was larger and encompassed the previous one. I was told the reason for that pattern was that they represented the growth of the city through the ages. They were the means of heavy transportation and formed a protective barrier against invasion. These water rings were connected to each other with spokelike links. There were, in fact, seventy canals within the city limits.

In the afternoon, I located the American Express and bought a ticket to Germany. I was told that it was a *sealed* train, and I puzzled over that description. In another few days, I would find out.

Late in the afternoon, I returned to my room to discover that all my roommates had also returned. We continued our bull session from the previous evening.

One of the boys picked up a pillow and let it fly across the room. In a flash, there was a super pillow fight in progress. This was great fun until one of the pillows burst. Now there was a dusty kapok substance all over the room.

The fun was definitely over. We considered our sure expulsion once the old landlady discovered our infraction of her strict rules. It's time for action. Someone produced a knife, and we split seams on the other pillows. We removed a portion of filling from each and filled the empty casing until they all looked similar. Two of the lads had little sewing kits, and we carefully refastened the pillowcase ends.

Now came the hard part: to clean up where the little piles of kapok littered the floor. We located a flat piece of cardboard that made a makeshift dustpan. Using a towel from the washroom, we wiped the dust on to the cardboard. An open window became a wonderful receptacle for this dusty mess. The problem was solved, and we were all in good humor once again.

On the way for our evening meal, we passed through the main lobby and made a startling discovery. The hotel patrons were coughing, sneezing, and many were suffering from watery red eyes. No one seemed to have any idea what the problem might be. The landlady was asking all kinds of questions to everyone. We judiciously remained silent and returned to our room for an investigation.

One of our group leaned out the window and started to laugh. Just below our third story window in an opening for the induction fan for the hotel air conditioning system.

The next day we were worried, but nothing was detected. We remain unscathed from our escapade.

Nine a.m. and I took a tram out to the edge of the Zeider Zee to the little fishing village of Volendam. It is located on the bay that cuts deep into Holland.

In 1912, the government built a barrier dam across the mouth of the bay so that there is now only a gentle lake in the heart of the Netherlands. Over the years, it is gradually being filled with earth to produce more useable land for cultivation. One sad note, the Germans broke the dikes and flooded a lot of the reclaimed land to prevent the Allies from traveling across the land. The dikes have been repaired but it will take several years before the salt residue subsides so that crops will grow once again.

There are many small villages on the edge of the water, and for centuries, the local inhabitants have made their living by fishing. Today I had a two-hour wait for a boat to take me to the island of Marken.

While I waited, I walked about two miles along the dike that marks the edge of the Zeider Zee. The small boat that would take me to Marken docks chugged into port as I completed my walk.

Once on board, it took less than an hour to arrive at the Marken quayside. My transport nudged in among the small fishing vessels that were tied to the docks. This small island clung to the distant past and the local people maintained their slow, measured ways of life. There was a charm to the bright dresses, wooden shoes, white-peaked hats that all the ladies wear. The effect was one of a Rembrandt painting in real time.

The population was busy going about their day's chores. I walked down the narrow alleys and could see women churning butter and hanging fish out to dry on outside racks. Now and then, I could hear the click of a loom shuttle in motion as I passed a small tidy home.

The village seemed totally self-sufficient. I couldn't help but wonder how long this quiet way of life would survive in our modern world. A quaint roadside inn provided a place to sit and have tea and cheese sandwiches for lunch. The lady proprietor spoke broken English, and so we carried on a conversation. Her family had lived in this house for several generations. During the war, the town was able to keep some supplies hidden from the Germans so they were able to subsist on a very spartan lifestyle.

She wanted me to know how much the Dutch people appreciated the British and Americans for the liberation of their homeland. She asked for information about my family and so we spent a pleasant time in dialog.

Late in the afternoon, I returned to my hotel-YMCA abode. Will the secret of the unknown cause of hay fever-like reactions be found out? Fortunately, the hotel guests seemed recovered, and not a word was spoken of the strange event. After dinner, I reviewed my plans to travel to Denmark the day after tomorrow.

In the morning, I began my last day of travel around Amsterdam. The first leg was a tourist-boat trip through the canals that crisscross and circle the town. The boat I rode on is a long, narrow, low affair.

The design allows travel along the narrow waterways and under the low bridges that permits vehicular travel throughout the city. The tour guide spoke perfect English to our group. There were about twenty people on board. Most were American and British GIs with a small number of business and foreign government people.

My seatmate was a GI who had been stationed in Germany. He was a year older than I was. I thought he must be typical of the young replacements that had arrived. They were here to allow the veterans of the recent conflict to return home so they can be mustered out of service.

The only comment I had was that he seemed so naïve about the present world affairs. He made comments like, "We can whip the Russians in ten days if they make a move."

It made me shudder to think what will become of this fellow if push comes to shove in the next few months. I supposed it would be like most wars that if he survived the first few weeks, he will learn fast enough to keep his head down.

Our tour guide gave an interesting monologue of the history of Amsterdam. He emphasized the part these canals had played in the defense of the town.

The last trip of the day was a walk to Rembrandt's home. It had been turned into a beautiful museum. There were many of his paintings and drawings on view. The painting that struck me the most was the *Changing of the Guard.*

I spent an hour touring the building. Paintings, etchings, and memorabilia covered the walls. Now it was time to return to my quarters. Tomorrow I start for Denmark.

CHAPTER 35

Sunday, March 14, 1948
Across Germany on to Denmark

The day was gray, overcast with a slight drizzle. We traveled across the Netherlands in an east-northeast direction. Small, clean villages dotted the countryside. There was very little evidence of the war. The train moved smoothly on the rebuilt right-of-way. Our only irritant was the coal smoke from the locomotive that infiltrated our carriage. I made the acquaintance of a girl from Palo Alto, California. We had a fine time comparing memories of our homes. She was a military dependent traveling to Hamburg to live with her father who was an army officer stationed in Germany. The usual exchange of addresses ended our visit.

The German border was crossed near Nordhorn. Now evidence of the war was everywhere. Bombed-out buildings and bomb craters followed the railroad tracks. This was supposed to be a sealed train but it was not. The idea was to have all the windows taped up with brown paper so that the passengers could not see out. Now the paper was torn down almost completely.

The train traveled through mile after mile of devastation. I observed a prison camp alongside the tracks. Hundreds of dejected German troops milled about in the light drizzle. They wore tattered military uniforms under dark gray overcoats. The train moved with a slow creak and groan as we passed over the makeshift track repairs.

In one location, there was a military mess detail feeding the troops. Several large caldrons were filled with what looked like watery soup just below our train windows. It was being ladled out to a long line of shuffling, disheveled soldiers. Each man had a tin cup that was filled as he passed the battered caldrons. These poor fellows gave the appearance of complete apathy.

Hostilities terminated in mid-1945; how I wonder can this state of affairs still be in effect. A short distance away can be seen row on row of tattered tents. I know the stories of the Nazi atrocities, but I also know that the average soldier is just a trapped human caught up in the political nightmare of his country. An older man who sat near me kept muttering, "Serves the dirty bastards right." He has probably suffered from the war, but it does not hit me as a humane treatment of mankind.

I think this vengeful attitude of a victor over a vanquished will keep the human species on the verge of extinction for centuries to come. Perhaps there is such a thing as Armageddon!

My train now moved in a northeasterly direction toward the city of Bremen in Lower Saxony. It had been a long, weary trip, and I dozed much of the way. I was hardly aware of our passage through the city in my state of stupor.

After another hour, we approached the city of Hamburg in a dark drizzle. Bomb damage became more pronounced as we moved forward at a slow pace over the unstable tracks.

The train came to a stop in the ruins of a grand train station. Outside, a PA system made announcements in French and English. "All passengers must now disembark with their luggage and prepare to walk."

Out of the dark shadows,—skeletal, bent old men appear to carry bags for those who needed help. We all climbed down from our coaches and looked at the devastation. The train terminal was a mass of twisted metal and collapsed masonry. The end of the rails were literally broken and twisted skyward.

A leader appeared and motioned us to follow him forward. Most of us lugged our own suitcases as we picked our way through the debris. The mist and drizzle that fell through the blown-out ceilings gave the place the feel of a haunted landscape.

We passed out of the wreckage and walked for twenty-five minutes before arriving at another destroyed station. On the far side of this pile of rubble, another locomotive stood chuffing in the silent rain.

We all clambered aboard to get out of the damp chill. There was a short wait while some of the late passengers struggled out of the gloom with their baggage. The passage through Hamburg and its scenes of devastation were just unreal. During the war, this city was exposed to fire bombing by a thousand aircraft in one night. Far more people died here than were lost in either Nagasaki or Hiroshima. The results of total war are a chilling sight to remember.

Leaving Hamburg, we traveled north for some time before turning north-northwest toward Jutland, Denmark. Not much to see in the gathering gloom. As we bridged over the Kiel Canal, we passed this point of interest. This famous 61-mile waterway was constructed in the late 1800s.

The purpose was to allow quick transit of the German high fleet between the Baltic Sea and the North Sea. After WW I the Treaty of Versailles internationalized the canal. When Hitler came to power, he repudiated the treaty, and once again, it was German-owned and controlled.

Since the end of WW II it was again made an international waterway. This shortcut across Germany saved time and money for the countries that shipped products from America and Western Europe to the Scandinavian countries. My seatmate gave me an interesting lecture on the importance of this canal.

He somehow was connected with the administration of this link between the seas. My trip from Campbell, California had been a continual exposure to events that I had never heard of previously.

I dozed as the train rattled further north. I woke with a start as we passed through Flensburg. A few minutes later, we stopped to have our travel documents observed at the Danish border. For unknown reasons, the inspectors singled me out, and I had to remove all the items from my barracks bag. In a few minutes, they returned all the gear to me, and as they did not speak English, they just waved me back to my seat.

I became a little tense, as I had no idea what they had been looking for. My seatmate laughed and said, "You can't tell what's on their minds in this part of the world."

CHAPTER 36

Tuesday, March 16, 1948, Life in the village of Hylard near Orsted, Denmark

Exhaustion is the price for a long day of travel. I discovered as we cross into Denmark that the train terminates for the day in the town of Padborg just across the border.

Fortunately, one of the clerks in the rail station spoke English, and I was told that the train does not depart for the north of Jutland until eight the following morning. Furthermore, I was informed that it would be another long day of travel before I reached my destination.

I stumbled out into the gathering dusk and located a small hotel nearby. I was so tired that I didn't even bother with supper but turned directly into my room for a night's rest.

Early in the morning, I found a small shop that sold cheese and twists of hard bread. I had not had time to change some dollars into Danish kroner, but the shop owner was happy to accept one U.S. dollar bill in payment.

The exchange rate must be favorable because he added a thick slice of ham to my stash of delicious food. I was so hungry that I thought, *Never has a breakfast tasted this wonderful.*

There were a few minutes available before train time so I took the opportunity to walk and stretch my legs. The town was clean and the people all seemed to have a purpose as they walked with a brisk gait as they went about their business.

The train ride north was across mile upon mile of perfectly flat country with many small lakes. I saw nothing that looked like heavy industry, just neat little farms. It was still the cold part of the year so we often saw farmers pitchforking great piles of hay to feed the cattle.

This was certainly a slow trip as we stopped every few miles to add more big containers of milk and casks that, I was told, were filled with butter. These people seemed to live slow and tranquil lives out on this distant prairie. It made sense that immigrants from this part of the world settle in Minnesota and Wisconsin because the terrain is so similar.

The big draw in the United States was that there is still fresh land to be had. Here all the land is owned and when the original occupant died, his land was divided among his children. The result was that the parcels of land have become smaller and smaller.

It was seven in the evening as I climbed down from the train. The all-day ride on wooden seats had left me stiff, sore, and tired. With instructions from the railroad agent, the local taxi driver delivered me to the person in my address book.

I received a terrible shock when I discovered that the person in my address book died *fifteen* years ago! There had to be some error as my aunt Leona, who sent me to this place, had received a letter last year from this cousin!

Back we went to the train station for further consultation. There followed half an hour of spirited conversation spread over several telephone calls. I could not understand a word but, at last, the agent smiled and said in English that I had been delivered to the wrong house. What a relief!

I arrived at the home of the Hagensens in the small village of Hyllard. The owners did not speak a word of English so they asked the local schoolteacher to come over for tea. They were a friendly elderly couple, and we had a good time becoming familiar with one another. The house was a small two-story affair and had the delightful smell of tanned leather.

Downstairs was a shop where Mr. Hagensen, who was the town leather craftsman, made harnesses, saddles, belts, and almost anything made of leather. Upstairs where we were having tea were the living quarters.

My hosts offered me milk. It had been a long time since I had fresh milk. After my second glass, they all had a good laugh at my enthusiasm over such a common item. With the help of the teacher, I explained my past months of living on the rough, and they could not have been more hospitable.

The interpreter departed for the evening. (He would return every afternoon in the days ahead to make sense of what had happened during the day.)

Mrs. Hagensen provided an excellent meal of green salad, fresh bread, and cheese. They realized that I was exhausted, and after a short time, showed me to my room. They fixed me a bed in a small side room that was full of household memorabilia. They had placed a mattress on the floor, but it was very comfortable. The stored items gave me pleasure in trying to guess what purpose the various old objects might have been used for. The room was lit with a coal oil lamp that flickered and gave off dancing shadows on the walls. I intended to get up and blow out the lamp, but alas, when I awoke the following morning, someone else had done the job for me.

This morning a friend of theirs arrived with a little car that rattled and backfired. He spoke a little broken English, and together we drove around the dirt country roads while he pointed out the small, neat farms of his neighbors.

One thing that caught my interest were the elaborate barns, each with a tall silo attached to the end of the building. My driver explained that in the long cold winters, the cows could be fed and housed without going out into the freeze of a North Sea blizzard. The last visit for the day was far out in the country.

We parked the car at a roadside and walked out into the distance toward a high pile of rocks. On arrival, we saw a small weathered signboard: "At this spot seven English airmen perished trying to land their crippled bomber. March 13, 1943."

There were seven grave markers and a large burnt section of the bomber in front of the location. The local people had come out and hand-carried the rocks to build this cairn as a memorial to these flyers.

My driver was quite emotional telling me of the loss of so many foreigners who came to help in the rescue of his small country. For me, it provided another point of reference to the sacrifices of so many to provide the outcome of World War II.

By the time we returned to my guest home in the village, I started to feel terrible. My throat was sore, and I was flushed and had a temperature. I decided that next morning I should start back for my aunt's home in England.

In sum, it seemed to me that the inhabitants of this part of the world led quiet lives within their strong religious faiths. They worked hard by day but found their enjoyment in family and church once the sun goes down. They could not have been more hospitable to a stranger who drops in from outer space. I shall always remember this small farm community in the middle of Jutland where the pace of life was so tranquil. It reminded me of my grandparents' remembrances of life at their Iowa farm (circa 1870).

CHAPTER 37

March 17, 1948,

North Sea crossing and on to Sutton, Surry

I departed Hyland early in the morning and spent seven miserable hours dozing on hard wooden train seats. My head ached while perspiration soaked my shirt. My throat was so sore it was difficult to talk. After seven hours of misery, I arrived in the seaport of Esbjerg on the North Sea.

Fortunately, there was only an hour's wait before the night boat for Dover, England, departed. I obtained a room with a bed to sleep in. There was one other man assigned to the second berth in the small, cramped compartment. I went in immediately and stretched out to sleep.

Unfortunately, once out of port, the sea was running high in a strong wind. Within a few minutes, my roommate was retching in our small sink, and the smell drove me out on deck. The cool air felt good on my hot forehead. I stood with feet wide apart as the ship rolled heavily, and I watched the ship's silvery wake stream out behind us in the moonlight.

I soon began to shake in the cool air and decided to return to my bunk. Despite the fowl air and the constant moans of my roommate, a deep, troubled sleep soon overtook me. I awoke several hours, later bathed in sweat but with more strength.

I left my compartment and located the public rooms that were almost empty. The towel rack in the restroom provided me with paper to dry off my body that was wet with perspiration. Once this chore was completed, I felt better, and the air in the large public room was pleasant compared to my quarters below. I sat in a lounge chair, sipping hot coffee as I watched the dawn break. In about half an hour, we were nosing into a Dover dock.

The train station was near at hand, and I was soon traveling toward downtown London. On my arrival at Victoria Station, it only took the time to walk to the train office and purchase a ticket out to Sutton before I was once again on my way. My throat was now so sore that it was difficult to even swallow hot coffee.

I departed the local train in Sutton and now had to walk up High Street to my aunt's house. My strength was ebbing fast, and I kept thinking, *I've got to make it; I've got to make it!* At last, I was knocking on the front door of her home.

Later, my cousins said that I walked through the door and dropped my barraks bag. Next, my eyes rolled up, and I collapsed face down in the hallway. There was quite a flap as my four cousins and my aunt had all they could do to drag me into a downstairs bed.

When I regained consciousness, their local physician was standing at my bedside. He said, "You have a temperature of 104 and a severe case of strep throat. You are most fortunate as I have my first batch of the new antibiotic, penicillin. (This wonder drug was developed near the end of World War II.)

Once again my luck had held out. The next week I spent in bed with periodic injections of the new drug. Within ten days, I was up and about with my strength regained.

While I was recuperating from my illness, I read in the newspaper that there would be an unveiling of a statue of Franklin Roosevelt. It was to stand in the gardens of Grosvenor Square in front of the American Embassy.

The dedication would be in two weeks. Once the time arrived, I took the train to London and found my way to the American Embassy. A huge crowd had assembled in the vicinity. I worked my way through the throng until I was three feet behind a line of standing dignitaries. You could imagine my surprise when I realized who these people were! To my left, not more then seven or eight feet away, stood King George VI and his wife, Elizabeth, The Queen Mother.

To their right were Eleanor Roosevelt and Winston Churchill. (They were within touching distance.) Next and last in the line were the two princesses, Elizabeth and Margaret.

I listened to Winston and Eleanor talk as we all stood looking out into the garden. There was a parachute draped over the statue and off to the side a large crane. Down from the crane there was a line attached to the chute. After a drum and bugle corps had given a crisp rendition, the parachute was raised free of the effigy . . . There followed a round of applause. I wanted to speak to Mr. Churchill but did not quite have the nerve. The event ended when the dignitaries were whisked away in huge shiny limousines.

A few days later, I went to the House of Commons to hear Mr. Churchill speak in a debate on the subject of capital punishment. This was a fascinating display of public speaking. I would listen to a pro or con on the subject and my mind would be swayed first one way and then the other. The oratory of these opposing politicians was extremely compelling.

When the final vote was taken, the English Empire abolished capital punishment. I was indeed fortunate to have been an observer of an event that changed British law that had stood for over a thousand years.

March progressed and the weather improved for my trips to airfields and foot tours of downtown London. The Tower of London was my favorite haunt as it is a fabulous museum of British history.

On another day, I took a trip out to Windsor Castle. On this junket, I committed a stupid teenage trick and was fortunate enough to escape with nothing more than a severe tongue-lashing.

While on tour down in the dungeons, I noticed a 2-foot key that was used to lock one of the iron cells. I decided to liberate this for a souvenir. I slid it down into my Levi's and walked out a little stiff legged.

All went well until I was halfway down the great marble steps that lead down from the castle door. With out warning, the key slid down my pant leg making a resounding clank as it hit the steps. In an instant, one of the guards that stood at the entrance was on me, and I had to relieve myself of my intended trophy. He marched me back into a side room where a stern looking man gave me a tongue-lashing. In the end, I was told to get on my way and "don't come back."

Back in my aunt's house, the morning papers were full of news regarding Russian saber rattling. My aunt's neighbors would often come by for tea and in a short time the conversation would turn to the Russians. There was a definite air of panic as the public considered the possibility of World War III. I decided the time had come for me to return to the United States.

One day, I met a man on one of my trips to the foreign shipping companies in search of a passage to the United States. This fellow explained that there was a way an American citizen could find a job aboard a U.S. ship without joining an expensive union.

The method was as follows: first, find some old clothes and let your beard grow; next, go to the American Embassy and explain that you are destitute and needed a job to return home.

I located a raggedy overcoat and a few other mismatched clothes and made my grimy appearance at the embassy. I told the clerk my story in a sad, pleading voice. He said, "Come back in a few days, and I will see what I can do."

I returned on April 15 after he had left a phone message at my aunt's home in Sutton. First, he checked my passport to see that all was in order and then asked if I could be in Southampton the following evening to take the place of a sailor who had jumped ship. The following afternoon, I took the train from London down to South Hampton.

CHAPTER 38

Evening of April 17 to Morning of April 25, 1948, Luxury liner across the Atlantic

Upon arrival at the docks in Southampton, I located the offices of the United States Lines. An official took my note from the American Embassy—London and delivered me to a small office on the dock beside the giant ocean liner USS *Washington*.

The next event left me a little shaken. I was introduced to a Mr. Rufus James. A swarthy black man, who I estimated to be at least six foot six, walked up and eyed me up and down for a full minute. Without a word, he walked over to me and grabbed my shirt at the neck and gave it a viscous twist. "Now get this, you little son of a bitch. I have to take you to replace another little jerk that jumped ship yesterday! You report to the chief porter. If one word of trouble regarding you reaches me, I will personally come down and beat the crap out of your scrawny body!" With his lecture over, he gave me a crew member's boarding pass and told me to report for work. More than a little unnerved, I left his presence and climbed the gangway in search of the chief porter.

Events turned for the better when I met the rotund chief porter. I gave him a short description of my trip from California. After looking over my papers, he started to laugh. "I presume you have met our jolly Mr. Rufus. You look like you could use a good meal. Stow your barracks bag forward in the utility men's bow quarters.

"Next, take one of the empty upper bunks. Then, go up to the mess hall for dinner. Report back in one hour."

Once in the crew mess hall, I could not believe my good fortune. There were three main courses, several kinds of fruit, and a variety of deserts to choose from. After a hearty meal washed down with cups of fresh, hot coffee, I was ready for my first work assignment.

I was put to work moving suitcases down into the hold for storage. It was amazing the size and amount of items some of these passengers were transporting. A few of the trunks were so heavy it was all that two of us could carry. We all worked hard for three hours and then we were through for the day.

Later the chief porter came by and said, "You'll do just fine." I had not seen him but he must have checked by to see if I would carry my share of the workload. It was late in the evening when I returned to my quarters. I took a hot shower and retired to my bunk.

The compartment lights were still on, and I observed other roommates get ready for rest. This observation was a little unsettling as most of the men were either black or Cuban, and they all spoke a singsong language that I could not understand.

Many of them carried scars that, in my imagination, must have come from knife fights. The item that put me off the most was that about half of them pulled out knives that they placed under their pillows before retiring. That first night I slept little and spent a lot of time out on deck. When I returned to my bunk, my mind would run rampant with the thought of being stabbed in my sleep.

In the twilight, the great ship's crew disengaged the mooring lines, and we sailed south-southeast into the Solent Channel to pass abeam of the Isle of Wight. Once clear of the island, we put about to a heading of southwest down the English Channel.

Our first port of call would be Cobh, Ireland. The ship passed Lands End, and we made for the southeast coast of Ireland. The ship's log produced these figures: "Arrived Cobh after a run of 15 hours and 22 minutes over a distance of 340 nautical miles on calm seas. The ship cruised at a speed of 22 knots."

The purpose of the stop in southern Ireland was to pick up several hundred immigrants en route to the United States. The lower half of Ireland had stayed neutral in the recent world war. The people suffered from the German blockade even though they were not belligerents. These people were a sorry lot of humanity.

Their clothes were little more than rags, and the effects of near starvation showed in their haggard faces. One poignant scene I shall never forget was that of a stooped old man leaning on the rail with tears that streamed down his weathered face. He repeated over and over in a sad, low voice, "Oh, my beloved Emerald Isle, I shall not live to see ye again."

The loading of ship's stores took only a short time. We took on baggage that was composed of bundles, bags, and even paper parcels of clothing. In less than three hours, we were off the Cobh dock and headed out to sea once again.

Once out into the Atlantic, the ship took on a gentle roll in the long swells that moved onto our port beam. As we got underway, these starving emigrants flooded below into the second-class restaurant to gorge on the rich food service. The results were predictable. Seasickness soon affected the majority and they walked around the public spaces throwing up. Trying to be helpful, they did not unload on the smooth floors where the mess could be easily cleaned up. No, the place of choice was the public drinking fountains. My boss rounded up a few of us minor crew members and assigned us the wonderful cleanup job.

One has not lived until he spends time trying to remove puke from the bottom of a drinking fountain. We were given canvas covers to lace down over the openings to prevent further use of these facilities after each one was carefully cleaned.

Yuck, what a job! The result was that, in the future, people got sick on the polished decks. The cleanup was accomplished with ease after a box of sawdust was spread on top and then swept into a dustpan. A quick mop with some disinfectant and the job was complete. I had to stop a time or two to settle my stomach so I went outside and stood in the cold, damp air that flowed across the deck and soon my head cleared.

After completion of this task, I was assigned a plum job. On a regular watch basis, I was told to spend my duty time walking the promenade decks cleaning up the minor debris that the first-class passengers left lying about the area. Odd bits of paper, Coke bottles, and cigar butts were deposited over the rail on the down wind side of the ship.

The result was a lot of time to visit with passengers. Business people, military officers, and a majority of well-to-do citizens all had their stories to tell. These people were on the cutting edge of the rebuilding of war-torn Europe. It would not be possible for me to stumble on to a more interesting short-term occupation. I spent the hours asking questions about the prospects of the future of Western Europe.

Because of the Marshall Plan, there predominated a sense of great hope. The one subject that worried all of them was what the Russians planed to do in the near future. This persistent concern left an edge of anxiety in my mind.

The days passed without incident, and I became friends with some of the rough men in my compartment. What a relief it was to sleep in complete confidence that I would not have my throat cut during the night. In the week that I spent with these men, there was not one incident of belligerence. Some of them certainly looked and acted sullen, but they were decent to me.

I made a point of not mentioning the cushy job to which I had been assigned. If they asked what I did, I would explain the fun of cleaning up after sick passengers, and that would put them into a gale of laughter. In the mess hall, some of them described their lives as ordinary seamen. For most, it was an improvement of their living standards. Having been born into a third world country, they had little education and few prospects of a decent living in their homeland. They jumped at the opportunity to live a maritime existence. This work provided them with good food, lodging, and spending money.

About 10:00 p.m. on April 23, we were transferring luggage from the hold up onto C deck to be ready for unloading on our arrival in New York City. The bags were stacked eight or ten high against an inner bulkhead. Without warning, the ship made a sudden turn to port which caused the wall of suitcases to cascade across the deck. The ship turned once again and the bridge officers turned out all the ship's lights. Not a sound came from the public address system. Next, there was a deep rumble as the ship's propellers were reversed and we shuddered to a dead stop and then all was deathly quiet. I had no idea what was going on!

I had departed Europe because war with the USSR was considered imminent and I wished to be home in the United States in the event that hostilities should break out. People throughout Western Europe were selling their property in panic. Many were shipping their valuables to the United States and Canada. It was a time of real concern as the United States started the "Berlin Airlift" to prevent the Russians from starving out Berlin. The newspapers were full of predictions of Armageddon.

Without any warning, the night was filled with the frightful roar of aircraft flying low over our ship. Then on a second pass, the planes dropped flares that lit us up with a bright halo on the dark sea. I was certain that WW III had started, and we were about to be torpedoed.

I had read enough stories about men dying in the freezing North Atlantic in WW II to put the fear of God into me. Being able to swim was not one of my abilities in this stage of my life. I was filled with anxiety as I made my way back to the fantail looking for something to cling to if the ship went down. I was certain that we would be sinking in the next few minutes.

Now the sound of the twin engine aircraft faded away and we just rolled in the mid-ocean swells without a sound. Then out of the blackness came three life rafts that paddled up to the side of our ship. Our ship's crew lowered a ladder down to sea level, and the airmen on board the rafts scrambled up into our ship. The lights came back on, and we were soon up to our 22-knot cruising speed.

The next day, I had an opportunity to talk to one of the ship's officers, and he explained the event. A B-25 bomber had ditched in the sea while the rest of his flight circled overhead and radioed a distress message. My ship, a twin screw, turbine steamer christened *S.S. Washington*, was the nearest vessel to the scene, and we were vectored to the rescue

The concern was that with such a large ship, we might run over the tiny life rafts in the dark. The solution was to shut off our ships lights so that the lookouts might be able to see the rafts. Next, the in-flight aircraft dropped flares so that we could see the survivors. Once the rafts were in sight, we stopped the ship dead in the water and let the downed fliers row up to us. No announcements were made because the captain of our ship was concerned that hundreds of the ship's passengers would rush up on deck and hinder the rescue operation.

The event ended with our arrival in New York City. Civilian and military bands were on hand to greet the arriving airman with great fanfare. News reporters scurried around, taking down information from officers and crew members that had witnessed the event. The late editions of the newspaper were full of pictures of the rescued airman, and the arrival of our ship.

I went down to the paymaster and received money for my few days of work. I should admit that the good food and conversation with passengers was more pleasure than work. My adventure on the high seas was over.

CHAPTER 39

April 24-June 3, 1948, Homeward bound

Once off the ship, I made my way to uptown Manhattan to find a room at the Sloan House for time to unwind with a good night's rest.

What a joy to be back in the United States! No more fumbling trying to figure out the exchange rate when purchasing food and items. There was no feeling like the pleasure of the return to one's homeland.

The following day, I went out to Yankee Stadium to see the Yanks beat the Boston Red Soxs, 5 to 4. Hot dogs and Coca Cola are American standard at the ball games. It was just great to be back.

Two days later, I hitchhiked down to New Windsor, Maryland, to visit with a few of the men that I had sailed with on the *Humanitos*. They had all returned to their farms in the area.

I made one trip with my friend, Ralph Lechtern, in the old Federal semi. We were out three days, picking up bundles of clothing that would be delivered to needy Italians in the months ahead. The time passed all too soon as we reminisced of our trips of the previous fall.

It was time to start for home. On a beautiful spring day, I was out on the road hitchhiking northwest.

Traveling through West Virginia, a fellow picked me up and regaled me with stories of life in the soft coal mines. I was intrigued and so decided to see if I could go down into one of these mines.

In the town of Scots Run, West Virginia, I climbed out of my ride and went to look for a place to stay for the night. Such local impoverishment brought back images of devastated towns in southern Europe.

There wasn't a town, just a general store run by the local coal-mining company. I went in and inquired for a place I might stay the night. A nice gray-haired lady suggested that I might walk back through the woods to a Presbyterian Mission called the Shack.

I located the weathered clapboard building set in a little clearing in the forest. Kevin Kendall was the minister who managed the place. He was attempting to improve racial conditions between the black and white miners.

Sadly, he had completed a year with no noticeable improvements. He did not seem discouraged and carried on.

"Yes." I could sleep in a cot in one corner of the main hall. This room was an interesting place. It was filled with rows of folding chairs. They all faced a wall with a large paper picture of Jesus Christ, and this became the mission church. If the chairs were all reversed to face the back wall, one could see a life-sized print of John L Lewis. In this mode, the building becomes a United Mine Workers union hall.

Later, the minister and his assistant, Clifford Nakatagawa, invited me to have dinner with them. It was plain fare—baked beans, cornbread, and a glass of milk—but to a hungry lad, it was just right.

We talked about world news and more about Lewis who the U.S. government was threatening with jail if he does not stop the general strike that had paralyzed this coal-mining region. Later, the Reverend Kendall said that tomorrow he would introduce me to a man who ran a jippo mine. This small mine was independent of the big mining company that ran most of the pits in these parts. It was still in operation because it was non-union.

Early the following morning, Big Earl, the owner of the jippo mine, arrived, and I followed him off through the woods. We traveled about a mile through the thick woods and gully until we arrived at his mine. Three rusty, dented pickup trucks were parked at the end of the rutted road that terminated at the mine. There were four men waiting for the boss, and they were introduced to me. After a discussion, one of the boys, who seemed to be the most educated of the lot, tore a piece of paper off his lunch bag and writes a message on it with a stub of a pencil. After a moment, he brought it over to me to sign. "I, Chuck Cutting, do not holt responsible the owner or employees of the "Dog Ears" mine if I should get hurt or kilt while underground in this here mine!!!!" I signed my name in a blank space.

He added the date, and all the men signed their names. I observed that one placed three X's for his signature. The owner took out a hammer and nailed this notice to a tree near the entrance to the mine.

Down we went through a long declining tunnel. Some places it was easier to go on hands and knees and other places we could walk bent over. The miner's lamps cast dim, eerie shadows on the broken walls.

Then, out of the gloom, I could make out a strange machine. They called it a "Joy Machine."

It was about four feet wide by six feet long. Mounted on caterpillar tracks, its top just grazed the ceiling. Out front was an arm with a continuous moving chain of cups with claw lips. They braced the machine to the sides and above with adjustable iron rods that they screwed tight into the walls. When they turned the electricity on, the noise was deafening as steel cups chattered against the face of the coal wall. Behind the device was a small trailer that rapidly filled with coal bits as the arm pushed forward. The air was thick with coal dust.

The miners wore no protective breathing devices and it was easy to see why so many men suffer from black lung disease. In a few minutes, the arm had reached its limit; and the machine was shut down and forced forward, locked down, and the cycle started once again.

While this was going on, two men worked the trailer, filled with coal, back out to the entrance dump. With the arrival of the first break, they were already black as the coal dust adhered to their sweat covered faces and arms. They all sat down to hand roll cigarettes and were soon puffing away. If cave-ins don't do them in, then the smoke and dust will destroy their lungs. It was amazing to see how others made their living. The importance of an education becomes very evident when viewed against the brutal work that a lot of mankind has to endure to provide food and lodging for their families.

By break time, I had seen enough and left after thanking them for their hospitality. The walk back through the clean forest air was delightful after those few hours in hell. How do they get men to do such work?

CHAPTER 40

June 3-June 18, 1948,
Returning to Campbell and on to college

On my return to the Shack, I packed my few items in my duffel bag and prepared to depart. Cliff, the assistant minister, came up to me and said he wanted to return to California and asked if I mind if he joined me?

I was well aware that hitchhiking with another person is much more difficult than doing it alone. Drivers are often afraid of a pair on the roadside, as skullduggery is more a possibility. Picking up two men means that one of them will be seated behind the driver where he is out of sight.

Cliff wanted to return to California, where his girlfriend waited his return from this assignment by the Presbyterian Church. I had talked at length with him the night before, and he seemed a decent man. "Okay," I said, "let's get going."

We decided to travel to Chicago where he had relatives. We actually made pretty good time on our trip to the Windy City. On arrival at 3853 South Lake Park, we were treated like royalty. Cliff's relatives were wonderful, hospitable people.

The second day after our arrival, I left for the day. This gave Cliff time to catch up on the family events while I went downtown to visit the Museum of Science and Industry. On my return, they had prepared a steak dinner with all the trimmings. I had the opportunity to talk with these folks and their neighbors, who joined us for the meal. They had been in a Japanese-American internment camp during the war. In the morning, we would leave these people for our continued journey west.

This morning, Cliff's cousin drove us out to the far western edge of Chicago and left us to try our luck on the road. In the next few days, we moved westward with more and more downtime at the side of the road. I was not positive, but I felt that because of the recent war in the Pacific; western people tended to be unfriendly toward my Asian friend.

For whatever reason, we stalled out in Omaha, Nebraska. After standing in the hot sun and blowing dust next to an abandoned filling station, Cliff came up with an idea.

In the distance, we could see a freight train a mile away as it made its slow acceleration out of a railroad switchyard. His suggestion? Why not try our hand at "riding the rails"?

With that thought in mind, we decided to give it a try. We hoisted our bags to our shoulders and climbed through a hole in the fence behind the filling station. When we had covered half the distance to the tracks, we observed another train with a long string of loaded cars pull out of the switchyards and begin its slow acceleration.

We listened to the tandem diesel engines produce a mournful howl that flooded out across the plain. If we were to make this string of cars, it was time to run. The terrain had looked smooth from the road but now we encountered large rocks, ditches, and patches of thick, dry weeds, all of which slowed our progress.

My 32-pound duffel bag chafed my neck while a stream of perspiration ran down between my shoulder blades. Abreast of the tracks, I halted and was surprised to see how close proximity changed the view. The pencil line of tracks now became ribbons of hard steel on top of a raised bed of broken rock. Rusty iron spikes secured the rails to an endless trail of rough, oil-stained crossties. Time did not allow further observation of the tracks.

The train bore down upon our position with a speed faster than we had calculated. The engine team swept by, and we ran as fast as possible along the rocky bed. My speed was still short of that needed to match the flatcar I had selected to board. It slipped ahead of me. The next dull brown car moved past, stains of a thousand-day's travel streaked its flanks.

My lungs began to burn from the intense effort. I saw the decals on the side of the flatcar, "Northwestern—Load Limit 179,000 LBS," move past, and realization hit, I must make a commitment now!

My strength will soon start to fade. With a determined effort, I threw my duffel bag onto the bed of the flatcar. Now with the reduced load and the added stability, I increased my speed to match that of the singing wheels.

I grasped an iron handhold at the end of the car and pull up onto the foot rung. For a moment of uncertain balance, my body swung half around toward the massive coupling that bound the car that followed.

I looked down to see the malignant, dull sheen of the rails and felt the steady beat of the double wheels. Balance regained, I climbed to the top of the bed and turn to see my friend Cliff. He was okay. Two cars back, he gave me the thumbs up, and I thought all was well.

At that instant, I was hit with another reality. From the car following him, a giant railroad bull appeared. He was swinging a long billy club back and forth as he moved up the car behind Cliff. I waved frantically to my companion to look behind him.

Fortunately, he looked back in time. We both threw our bags off into the sage and climbed down on the foot rungs and jumped off on the run. The train had gathered more speed in the minutes since we boarded, and it was too much for us to handle. I ran as hard as I could but I can't keep my footing under me, and down I fall into the sage and dry grass along the right-of-way.

I lay breathing heavily and felt to see if I was hurt. The skin on one arm and my chest were scraped to a reddish color, but otherwise, I seemed intact. After a few moments, I gathered my strength and got up off the ground, wincing with the pain. I looked back down the track to see Cliff moving his hands over his rib cage. We both picked up our duffel bags and walked to join each other. We sat for a few minutes and congratulated each other on our narrow escape. This was the end of our attempt to ride the rails out west.

In a short time, we were back beside the abandoned gas station. The sun had grown hotter and a steady breeze pushed dust in, off the prairie. It did not take long before our scrapes began to weep. The dust-laden air soon caked our broken skin with a dirty layer.

We were trying to hitchhike, but I swore that when drivers saw our condition, they not only passed without stopping, but they also appeared to accelerate.

We spent a miserable hour with no result when, at last, a big semitruck pulled up alongside and provided us with a ride. The driver's first words were, "You fellows must have been in a hell of a fight." He thought it's hilarious when we told him of our aborted train ride.

All my joints ached and my head throbbed as we rolled on toward the Colorado border. Our benefactor was en route to Denver. We arrived in this western town late in the night. Once out of the truck, we located a cheap hotel to rest for the night.

On the western outskirts of town the next morning, we stood out in the rising sun looking for a ride. It wa noon before we caught another truck that would deposit us in Delta, Utah. Once there, we sat by the roadside and talked about possibilities.

In the end, we were both anxious to reach California and decided to pool our money and locate a bus station. We came up with just enough money to buy two greyhound tickets to San Jose. We piled into a bus and slumped in a stupor and let the miles roll past.

In the afternoon of June 18, 1948, I had completed my journey and arrived back in my grandparents' home in Campbell, California.

I began this trip in September 1947 with four hundred dollars. I was now monetarily broke, but in exchange, I had transited from youth into adulthood.

EPILOGUE

In that summer of long ago, I returned to work for Nelson Brothers Trucking Company as a semitruck driver. With the proceeds from the summer, I enrolled in San Jose State University in the Aeronautical Department. In the years ahead after collage graduation, I worked two years as a flight test engineer for Douglas Aircraft Company. This was followed by a thirty-five-year career with Pan American World Airways. I started as a flight engineer flying over the Pacific Ocean in Boeing Stratocrusiers. My airline career concluded at age sixty as the captain of Boeing 747s, crisscrossing the world's air routes.

My interest in world events and history was augmented with the opportunity to visit many places that I had visited in 1947-48. I also had the good fortune to spend a three-year tour domiciled in Berlin, Germany. That trip to Europe as a teenager set the stage for my life of exploring the world of ideas, events, and fascinating people.

One sad note from the cross-country trip home in 1948 concerned my friend, Clifford Nakatakawa. After we had parted company in San Jose, he continued on to live with his relatives in Stockton. He completed his education and sent occasional notes of support and interest. One year, I did not receive a card during Christmas season, and after a time, I contacted his relatives to receive the sad news. One night, returning from a church function, driving home on Highway 99, a drunk careened across the center divider and crashed head on into their car. My friend, his wife, and their small child all died in the ensuing crash.

Life is such a transient event that I believe we should grasp on to and make the most of every day we are given. Listen to all that pass our way and learn from them the lessons of their lives.